# Facebook
## The Missing Manual

# Facebook: The Missing Manual, First Edition   BY E. A. VANDER VEER

Published by O'Reilly Media, Inc., 1005 Gravenstein Highway North, Sebastopol, CA 95472.

O'Reilly books may be purchased for educational, business, or sales promotional use. Online editions are also available for most titles (*safari.oreilly.com*). For more information, contact our corporate/institutional sales department: 800.998.9938 or corporate@*oreilly.com*.

**Executive Editor:** Peter Meyers

**Editor:** Dawn Frausto

**Production Editor:** Nellie McKesson

**Copy Editor:** Jill Steinberg

**Indexer:** Julie Hawks

**Cover Designer:** Karen Montgomery

**Interior Designer:** Ron Bilodeau

**Print History:**

January 2008:        First Edition.

ISBN-10: 0-596-51769-6
ISBN-13: 978-0-596-51769-4

[F]

# Contents

## Part 1: From Signing Up to Staying Connected

### Chapter 1

### Chapter 2

### Chapter 3

### Chapter 4

**Chapter 5**

# Part 2: Interest Groups and Shopping

**Chapter 6**

**Chapter 7**

**Chapter 8**

# Part 3: Doing Business with Facebook

**Chapter 9**

# Part 4: Privacy and Power Tools

# Part 5: Appendix

# The Missing Credits

## About the Author

**E. A. Vander Veer** started out in the software trenches, lexing and yaccing and writing shell scripts with the best of them. She remained busy and happy for years writing C++ programs and wresting data from recalcitrant databases. After a stint as an Object Technology Evangelist (yes, that's an actual job title), she found a way to unite all of her passions: writing about cool computer stuff in prose any human being can understand. Books followed—over a dozen so far—including *PowerPoint 2007: The Missing Manual, Javascript for Dummies, XML Blueprints*, and the fine tome you're holding right now. She lives in Texas with her husband and daughter. Email: *emilyamoore@rgv.rr.com*.

# About the Creative Team

**Dawn Frausto** (editor) is assistant editor for the Missing Manual series. When not working, she likes rock climbing, playing soccer, and causing trouble. Email: *dawn@oreilly.com*.

**Peter Meyers** (editor) is the managing editor of O'Reilly Media's Missing Manual series. He lives with his wife, daughter, and cats in New York City. Email: *peter.meyers@gmail.com*.

**Nellie McKesson** (production editor) is a graduate of St. John's College in Santa Fe, NM. She currently lives in Cambridge, MA, where her favorite places to eat are Punjabi Dhaba and Tacos Lupita. Email: *nellie@oreilly.com*.

**Keith McNamara** (editorial assistant) is a former Marine and graduate of the University of Connecticut. He currently works at O'Reilly wearing multiple hats, including production for the Missing Manual series. Email: *keithmc@oreilly.com*.

**Jill Steinberg** (copy editor) is a freelance writer and editor based in Seattle, and has produced content for O'Reilly, Intel, Microsoft, and the University of Washington. Jill was educated at Brandeis University, Williams College, and Stanford University. Email: *saysjill@mac.com*.

**Mark J. Levitt** (technical reviewer) is the online manager for conferences at O'Reilly Media. He's a Facebook and general social networking enthusiast whose background includes computer science, interactive media, and Web development. He's known to eat cereal at all hours of the day. Email: *mark@levittation.com*.

**Matthew Roberts** (technical reviewer) is a software engineer for the IT Department at O'Reilly Media, Inc. His leisure time is unevenly divided between consuming art and creating it. Email: *matt@oreilly.com*.

**Tina Spargo** (technical reviewer), her husband (and professional musician) Ed, their toddler Max, their two silly Spaniels, Parker (Clumber), and Piper (Sussex), all share time and space in their suburban Boston home. Tina juggles being an at-home mom with promoting and marketing Ed's musical projects and freelancing as a virtual assistant. Tina has over 15 years' experience supporting top-level executives in a variety of industries. Web site: *www.tinaspargo.com*.

# Acknowledgments

*Muchísimas gracias* to the Missing Manual editorial team—y'all truly are second to none. Special thanks go to Pete Meyers for suggesting this book, and for overseeing the entire process with wisdom and grace. Dawn Frausto's top-notch editing buffed the manuscript to a high sheen, and tech reviewers Mark Levitt, Matt Roberts, and Tina Spargo triple-checked it for accuracy and currency (no mean feat when you're writing about a Web site so popular it spits out new features faster than Hollywood spits out buddy movies). A smart, nimble team like this one is every writer's dream.

# The Missing Manual Series

Missing Manuals are witty, superbly written guides to computer products that don't come with printed manuals (which is just about all of them). Each book features a handcrafted index; cross-references to specific pages (not just chapters); and RepKover, a detached-spine binding that lets the book lie perfectly flat without the assistance of weights or cinder blocks.

Recent and upcoming titles include:

*Access 2007: The Missing Manual* by Matthew MacDonald

*AppleScript: The Missing Manual* by Adam Goldstein

*AppleWorks 6: The Missing Manual* by Jim Elferdink and David Reynolds

*CSS: The Missing Manual* by David Sawyer McFarland

*Creating Web Sites: The Missing Manual* by Matthew MacDonald

*Digital Photography: The Missing Manual* by Chris Grover and Barbara Brundage

*Dreamweaver 8: The Missing Manual* by David Sawyer McFarland

*Dreamweaver CS3: The Missing Manual* by David Sawyer McFarland

*eBay: The Missing Manual* by Nancy Conner

*Excel 2003: The Missing Manual* by Matthew MacDonald

*Excel 2007: The Missing Manual* by Matthew MacDonald

*FileMaker Pro 8: The Missing Manual* by Geoff Coffey and Susan Prosser

*FileMaker Pro 9: The Missing Manual* by Geoff Coffey and Susan Prosser

*Flash 8: The Missing Manual* by E.A. Vander Veer

*Flash CS3: The Missing Manual* by E.A. Vander Veer and Chris Grover

*FrontPage 2003: The Missing Manual* by Jessica Mantaro

*GarageBand 2: The Missing Manual* by David Pogue

*Google: The Missing Manual, Second Edition* by Sarah Milstein, J.D. Biersdorfer, and Matthew MacDonald

*The Internet: The Missing Manual* by David Pogue and J.D. Biersdorfer

*iMovie 6 & iDVD: The Missing Manual* by David Pogue

*iMovie '08 & iDVD: The Missing Manual* by David Pogue

*iPhone: The Missing Manual* by David Pogue

*iPhoto 6: The Missing Manual* by David Pogue and Derrick Story

*iPhoto '08: The Missing Manual* by David Pogue and Derrick Story

*iPod: The Missing Manual, Sixth Edition* by J.D. Biersdorfer

*JavaScript: The Missing Manual* by David Sawyer McFarland

*Mac OS X: The Missing Manual, Tiger Edition* by David Pogue

*Mac OS X: The Missing Manual, Leopard Edition* by David Pogue

*Microsoft Project 2007: The Missing Manual* by Bonnie Biafore

*Office 2004 for Macintosh: The Missing Manual* by Mark H. Walker and Franklin Tessler

*Office 2007: The Missing Manual* by Chris Grover, Matthew MacDonald, and E.A. Vander Veer

*Office 2008 for Macintosh: The Missing Manual* by Jim Elferdink

*PCs: The Missing Manual* by Andy Rathbone

*Photoshop Elements 6: The Missing Manual* by Barbara Brundage

*PowerPoint 2007: The Missing Manual* by E.A. Vander Veer

*QuickBase: The Missing Manual* by Nancy Conner

*QuickBooks 2008: The Missing Manual* by Bonnie Biafore

*Quicken 2008: The Missing Manual* by Bonnie Biafore

*Switching to the Mac: The Missing Manual, Leopard Edition* by David Pogue

*Switching to the Mac: The Missing Manual, Tiger Edition* by David Pogue and Adam Goldstein

*Wikipedia: The Missing Manual* by John Broughton

*Windows 2000 Pro: The Missing Manual* by Sharon Crawford

*Windows XP Home Edition: The Missing Manual, Second Edition* by David Pogue

*Windows Vista: The Missing Manual* by David Pogue

*Windows XP Pro: The Missing Manual, Second Edition* by David Pogue, Craig Zacker, and Linda Zacker

*Word 2007: The Missing Manual* by Chris Grover

The "For Starters" books contain only the most essential information from their larger counterparts—in larger type, with a more spacious layout, and none of the more advanced sidebars. Recent titles include:

*Access 2003 for Starters: The Missing Manual* by Kate Chase and Scott Palmer

*Access 2007 for Starters: The Missing Manual* by Matthew MacDonald

*Excel 2003 for Starters: The Missing Manual* by Matthew MacDonald

*Excel 2007 for Starters: The Missing Manual* by Matthew MacDonald

*PowerPoint 2007 for Starters: The Missing Manual* by E.A. Vander Veer

*Quicken 2006 for Starters: The Missing Manual* by Bonnie Biafore

*Windows Vista for Starters: The Missing Manual* by David Pogue

*Windows XP for Starters: The Missing Manual* by David Pogue

*Word 2007 for Starters: The Missing Manual* by Chris Grover

# Introduction

**M**aybe a Facebook invitation showed up in your email inbox and you're trying to decide whether to join the site. Maybe you were alarmed when you heard your kids mention *poking* each other on Facebook. Or maybe the Wall Street buzz caught your attention when Facebook—a whippersnapper of a Web site that didn't even exist until 2004—clocked in at a breathtaking value of $15 *billion*.

However you heard about it, everybody seems to be talking about Facebook. And for good reason: In an astonishingly short period of time, Facebook has grown from an online yearbook for college kids to an Internet juggernaut with over 50 million members.

So what *is* Facebook, anyway? It's a free-to-use, wildly popular social networking site—which means it's a way to connect with other people—that combines the best of blogs, online forums and groups, photo sharing, and much more. By tracking the connections its members make with each other, Facebook makes it easy to find and contact people—everyone from old friends and roommates to new customers, new bosses, and even folks you've never met before who share your interests.

> **Note** If you're thinking that Facebook sounds a lot like MySpace, you're right. The difference? In a word, positioning. Facebook does pretty much the same stuff as MySpace, but in a cleaner, more controlled, more professional way. So while MySpace's blinking, flashing, online teen haven boasts nearly twice as many members as Facebook, Facebook's membership is rapidly catching up. And over half of all new Facebook members count themselves among the 25-and-older crowd, so it's not just for college kids anymore.

# How Facebook Works

First, you type in your personal and professional information—as much or as little as you're comfortable with. (Most folks add extras such as photos, videos, and audio clips.) Then, you establish connections with groups of Facebook members, like everybody who went to your alma mater, or everybody who works at your company. Finally, you add individual connections to other members, such as the guys on your soccer team, your next-door neighbor, and the two or three old flames you're still speaking to. Bingo: instant access to the personal and professional details of all the folks you're connected to, and the folks *they're* connected to, and so on. You can think of Facebook as a 50-million-plus-entry searchable Rolodex—on steroids.

The two parts of the site you interact with most often are:

- **Your profile.** Your profile is the page that other Facebook members—friends, family members, co-workers, long-lost roommates, potential bosses, and so on—see when they look you up on Facebook (you can, of course, view your own profile, too). The *mini-feed* (page 80) on your profile makes it easy for your friends to see what you're up to. The figure below shows a sample profile.

- **Your home page.** The majority of your Facebook home page is taken up by a *news feed* (page 78) that chronicles your friends' Facebook activities. The right side of the page shows you stuff you might want to take action on: requests your friends have made, upcoming birthdays, and so on. It also lists any requests—to befriend someone or to install an application (page 206) one of your friends found useful, for example—that require your attention. To get to your home page, click the word "facebook" in the top-left corner of any Facebook screen, or click the "home" link in the upper right. Page xvi shows you what a typical home page looks like.

# What You Can Do With Facebook

Like all social networking sites, Facebook blurs the line between personal and professional: Your boss is just as likely as your kids to be on Facebook. Still, most folks focus on either professional or personal stuff when they're on the site. The following sections list some of the things you can do on Facebook.

## Social Activities

Facebook began life as a social networking site for college kids (it was started by a Harvard student), and personal interactions are still the main reason people sign up. You can:

- **Look up (and be looked up by) long-lost pals.** Facebook wouldn't be very useful if no one used their real names—you wouldn't be able to find anybody! But since it's fun to find people and have them find you (and because Facebook's official policy requires truthfulness), members tend to provide their real names, photos, and personal details. Chapter 3 teaches you how to search for people on Facebook.

- **Make new friends.** Facebook makes it easy to search out and contact folks with similar interests, whether you like Pedro Almodóvar movies or are frustrated with Geometry 102. And because your personal info is available for other Facebook members to see, you can learn a little about someone before you decide to contact or befriend him. Online special-interest *groups* (page 103) let you exchange views with like-minded Facebook members, and *events* (page 119) let you arrange face-to-face meetings with other members.

- **Keep in touch with far-flung friends and family.** Other Facebook members can sign up for regular updates from you. For example, you can send out party updates to fellow students stuck in study hall, or photos of your new granddaughter. Likewise, you can sign up to get updates about what your friends and family members are doing. Chapter 5 teaches you all about automatic updates.

- **Make yourself heard.** Facebook's blogging feature (called *notes*— page 90) lets you put text and photos on your profile. Think online journal—on steroids.

- **Buy and sell stuff.** *Marketplace* (page 131), Facebook's answer to classified ads, lets you buy and sell stuff online using a credit card (see Chapter 8).

- **Keep tabs on your kids.** Facebook started out as a way for students to meet online, and it's still big with college and high school kids. Getting acquainted with Facebook not only helps you understand the language your kids are speaking; it also gives you a frank look into their online social lives.

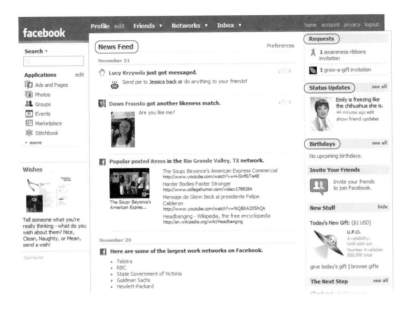

# Professional Uses for Facebook

You don't have to be out of work to benefit from social networking. More and more professionals are turning to Facebook to mingle, headhunt, advertise, and work more effectively. Here are some of the work-related things you can do on Facebook:

- **Find a gig.** The resumé you post on Facebook can be as extensive as you want (headhunters use Facebook, too), and there's always the want ads in Facebook's *Marketplace* (page 131). But because jobs often go to the best-qualified friend-of-a-friend, Facebook's ability to show you who's friends with who—maybe one of your friends knows the hiring manager—can be even more useful.

- **Find an employee.** Facebook can help you recruit new hires and even vet them (see Chapter 9).

- **Keep up-to-date on team projects.** Subscribing to *feeds* (page 78) and *notifications* (page 81) keep you in the loop regarding upcoming deadlines and other details, such as whether team members on the other side of the building are still online or have left for the day.

- **Collaborate.** Use Facebook's *walls* (page 67), *notes* (page 90), and *groups* (page 103) to exchange ideas, photos, and more; *messages* (page 60) to send email; and *events* (page 119) to schedule meetings and lunch dates.

- **Market yourself, your products, or your company**. For relatively little scratch, Facebook gives you several ways to promote things:

  - **Pages** are special interactive profiles for companies, bands, celebrities, and nonprofit organizations, and you can create them for free.

  - **Social ads** can include graphics and text; they appear in Facebook's ad space (the lower-left part of any screen), as well as in selected members' news feeds.

  - **Polls** are questions you can ask specifically targeted members.

  Big-bucks sponsor companies have even more marketing options. Chapter 11 explains all your choices.

# About This Book

Facebook is a terrifically fun and useful site, and compared to a lot of other Web sites, it's remarkably easy to use. But that's true only *if* you already know what you want to do on Facebook, and—most important—why.

That's where this book comes in. This is the book you *should* have been able to download when you registered for Facebook. It explains what kinds of things you can do on Facebook, and how to go about doing them. You'll find tips for diving headfirst into Facebook without looking like a newbie, keeping in touch with your friends, expanding your social circle, and using Facebook as a poor man's business collaboration tool. This book also guides you through the staggering forest of privacy options so you can get the most out of Facebook with the least amount of risk (see Chapter 13).

This book is designed for readers of every skill level, from I-just-plugged-in-my-first-computer-yesterday to Internet expert. Concise intros lead you into step-by-step instructions of how to get stuff done. The Notes scattered throughout the text give you alternatives and additional info, and the Tips help you avoid problems.

# Missing Manuals on Facebook.com

You can find Missing Manuals own home on Facebook by typing *Missing Manuals* into the Search box in the upper-left of any Facebook screen. Use the Page's *wall* (page 67) or *discussion board* (page 107) to post feedback about this book or any Missing Manual. And the Page is a great place to meet other folks who are fans of Missing Manuals—or to become a fan yourself (see page 187).

# About MissingManuals.com

At the *missingmanuals.com* Web site, you'll find articles, tips, and updates to this book. Click the "Missing CD-ROMs" link, and then click this book's title to see a neat chapter-by-chapter list of all the Web sites mentioned in these pages.

You're invited and encouraged to submit corrections and updates for this book. In an effort to keep it as up-to-date and accurate as possible, each time we print more copies of this book, we'll make any confirmed corrections you've suggested. We'll also note such changes on the Web site, so you can mark important corrections in your own copy of the book, if you like. (Click the book's name, and then click the "View/Submit Errata" link to see the changes.)

In the meantime, we'd love to hear your suggestions for new books in the Missing Manual line. There's a place for that on the Web site, too, as well as a place to sign up for free email notification of new titles in the series.

While you're online, you can also register this book at *www.oreilly.com* (you can jump directly to the registration page by going here: *http://tinyurl/ yo82k3*). Registering means we can send you updates about this book, and you'll be eligible for special offers like discounts on future editions of *Facebook: The Missing Manual*.

# Safari® Books Online

**Safari** ⋯▸ When you see a Safari® Books Online icon on the cover of your favorite technology book, that means the book is available online through the O'Reilly Network Safari Bookshelf.

Safari offers a solution that's better than e-Books. It's a virtual library that lets you easily search thousands of top tech books, cut and paste code samples, download chapters, and find quick answers when you nee the most accurate, current information. Try it free at *http://safari.oreilly.com*.

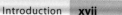

**1**

# Getting Started

**G**oogle, the iPod, spam: Only a handful of technological forces have gone from tiny to towering seemingly overnight, and Facebook can now join this elite crowd. One big reason: Setting up a Facebook account couldn't be easier. In the time it takes to say "howdy," you too can be part of the frenzy.

Then—if you like—you can fill out an optional Facebook *profile*, a series of questions regarding your likes, dislikes, educational and professional background, and so on. You can even include photos of yourself. The more accurately and completely you describe yourself to Facebook, the more useful you'll find the site. (After all, headhunters and old college buddies can't find you if you fake your information.) This chapter shows you how to sign up for an account, fill out your profile, and get to your personalized Facebook home page.

> **Tip** Of course, the more information you give Facebook, the more risk you take that someone will steal or misuse that information. See Chapter 13 for ways to get the most out of Facebook while minimizing your risk.

# Signing Up for an Account

Facebook accounts are free, and have only two requirements: You need a working email address, and you have to be over 13 years old. Here's how to sign up:

1. **Point your favorite Web browser to www.facebook.com.** If you're on a Windows computer, you'll get best results with Internet Explorer or Firefox. If you're on a Mac, use Firefox or Safari. (If you're not familiar with Firefox, check out *www.firefox.com*.)

> **Tip** You probably don't want to sign up for Facebook using your cellphone—there's quite a bit of typing involved—but in a pinch you can; see Chapter 14.

2. **Click the green Sign Up button.**

3. **Fill out all the fields on the Sign Up page that appears.** Facebook doesn't let you skip any fields, but you can change your answers later (page 19).

   - **Full Name.** Facebook expects you to use your real name, not an alias. Don't type in the name of a group or company, and don't include special characters (like parentheses) or titles such as Mr., Ms., or Dr.

     If you like, after you finish the sign-up process you can add your maiden name to your account so people you knew before you got hitched can find you. To do so: At the top of any Facebook page, click the "edit" link, and then click the Relationships tab and type your full maiden name in the Former Name field. Click the Save Changes button when you're done.

## Sign Up and Start Using Facebook

Join Facebook to **connect with your friends**, share photos, and **create your own profile**. Fill out the form below to get started (all fields are required to sign up).

Full Name:

I am:
- in college/graduate school
- at a company
- in high school
- none of the above

Email:

Password:

Date of Birth: Month: ▼  Day: ▼  Year: ▼

Security Check: Enter **both** words below, separated by a **space**. What's This?
Can't read this? Try another.

those ances

Text in the box:

☐ I have read and agree to the Terms of Use and Privacy Policy.

Sign Up Now!

Problems signing up? Go here.

---

**Tip** For the most part, it's up to you whether or not you give Facebook accurate personal details. But Facebook actually uses a combination of computer programs and real, live humans to weed out obviously bogus registration details. Type in Elvis Presley or Mickey Mouse for your full name, for example, and there's a good chance your registration won't go through.

- **I am.** Choose "in college/graduate school" or "in high school" and you'll be asked for more info, including graduation year and the email address associated with your school. Choose "at a company" and you'll need to type in your work email address. Choose "none of the above" if you don't have a valid school- or work-related email address.

**Tip** If you're worried about identity theft, you can get a free email address from a site such as *www.yahoo.com* or *www.google.com* to use with Facebook (instead of using an actual school- or work-related email address). But this anonymity will cost you: Only folks with valid school and work addresses can join school- and work-related *networks* (page 23).

- **Email.** This is your primary account email, so you need to make sure you type in a working email address. If you don't, you won't receive the confirmation message Facebook sends you, and therefore won't be able to complete the sign-up process. If you're interested in joining your employer's or school's Facebook *network* (page 23), use your employee email address (*kris_kringle@acme.com*) or your student email address (*kris_kringle@asu.edu*), respectively.

> **Tip** You can add additional email addresses to your account later, if you like—see page 30.

- **Password.** Make up a six-character or longer, case-sensitive password (you can use numbers, letters, or punctuation), and then jot it down in a notebook or some other safe place so you don't forget it.

- **Date of Birth.** Make sure the year you choose puts you over age 12— Facebook doesn't let under-13s use the site.

- **Security Check.** If you wait too long to type in the words that appear right above this field—say you get called away from your computer and leave the half-finished Sign Up page overnight—Facebook may refresh the words and ask you to type in the new ones.

- **Terms of Use checkbox.** Ideally, you should click both the Terms of Use link and the Privacy Policy link and read both of them before you turn on this checkbox. In reality, though, you'd need three hours and a law degree to make sense of them. And because Facebook reserves the right to change them any time it gets the urge, you'd have to keep re-reading them every day. So just put a check mark in the box.

> **Tip** Here's the gist of Facebook's Terms of Use and Privacy Policy: Be nice (don't spam anybody or post pirated stuff), be honest (leave out personal details if you must, but make sure the details you *do* give Facebook are accurate), and don't blame Facebook for anything bad that might happen (your office Christmas party pictures ending up in *National Enquirer* after you post them on Facebook, for example). Break these rules, and Facebook reserves the right to refuse you service.

4. **Click the "Sign Up Now!" button.** If you forgot to fill out any of the fields, you'll see the Sign Up page again, this time with a message at the top that reads, "You must fill in all of the fields." If you filled everything in to Facebook's satisfaction, then you'll see a confirmation box.

**Confirm Your Email Address**

Thanks for signing up! We just sent you a confirmation email to
**eamoore68@gmail.com.**

Click on the confirmation link in the email to complete your sign up.

Go to Gmail now

5. **In the confirmation box, click the "Go to" button, or just open your email program the way you usually do.** Either way, in your email inbox you'll find a message from Facebook asking you to confirm that you want to join.

**Tip** Facebook's pretty quick about responding to registration requests. Typically, the automated confirmation email shows up in your inbox within a couple of minutes.

Facebook <register@facebook.com> to n show details 11:20 am (1 hour ago) ↩ Rep

Hey Emily,

You recently registered for Facebook using this email address. To complete your registration. follow the link below:

http://www.facebook.com/c.php?code=499227856&rt=2&email=eamoore68%40gmail.com
(If clicking on the link doesn't work, try copying and pasting it into your browser.)

If you did not register for Facebook, please disregard this message.
Please contact info@facebook.com with any questions.

Thanks,
The Facebook Team

6. **In your email program, click the confirmation email's link (or cut-and-paste the link into your Web browser).** Bingo: Facebook displays a welcome message on your newly created, personalized Facebook home page. Congratulations—you're officially registered! (You're automatically logged in, too.)

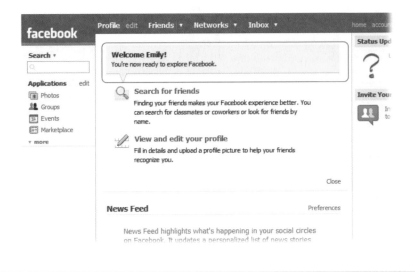

**Tip** After you register, the generic Facebook home page changes to one that's personalized just for you. The green Sign Up button you saw before you were a logged-in member disappears, and in its place you see links to useful things you can do in Facebook, like search for friends who are already Facebook members (page 36) and view and edit your Facebook profile (page 7).

# Creating Your Profile

A Facebook *profile* is a collection of facts about you: everything from where you went to school and how old you are, to what kind of romantic relationship you're in (or hope to be in) and your favorite TV shows. All your Facebook friends and fellow network members can see your profile details (except for the Facebook members you explicitly exclude; see Chapter 13).

Facebook automatically creates a bare-bones profile for you based on the info you entered when registering. Whether or not you add additional details—and how much you add—is up to you.

**Tip** If you *do* decide to flesh out your profile, brevity and truthfulness pay off by helping Facebook connect you with like-minded folks. That's because Facebook automatically lists your profile answers in the search results other members see. The site can also suggest potential "friends" by matching your profile answers with those of other members (see Chapter 3).

When polishing your profile, ask yourself:

- **What do I want to get out of Facebook?** If you just want to check out your ex-spouse's Facebook profile, you don't need to waste time crafting one of your own. But if you hope to use Facebook to do some networking and land a job, spending some time and effort building your profile is definitely worth the effort.

- **How security-conscious am I?** Although Facebook's success is based, in part, on its scrupulous commitment to member privacy, the sad truth is that everything you put on the Internet is subject to possible misuse and theft—including what's in your Facebook profile. Think twice about including political, religious, sexual, and other sensitive proclivities unless revealing these details is absolutely necessary. For example, if you registered for Facebook specifically to connect with other political activists in your area, fill out the political section of your profile. Otherwise, skip it.

- **How much time do I want to spend on this?** Profile building can be a huge time suck. If you're anxious to start using Facebook, just add a few details now. You can always add more later (page 8).

**Tip** If all you add to your profile is one detail, make it a flattering picture of yourself. Doing so is quick, easy, and lets folks who already know you identify you right off the bat—even if your name is John Smith.

## Viewing Your Profile

Taking a look at your profile from time to time is a good idea, because it lets you see yourself as other Facebook members see you.

To view your profile:

1. **Make sure you're registered (page 2) and logged in (page 5).**

**Tip** If you just finished registering by clicking the link in the confirmation email (page 5), you're already logged in.

2. **Head to the top of any Facebook screen and click Profile.**

The profile that appears shows all the information you've given Facebook. If you've just registered, the only details you see are the bare-bones ones Facebook got from you during the registration process.

## Adding Basic Information

Most of the information Facebook categorizes as "basic" really isn't all that useful. You'll probably just want to type in your hometown and country information and skip the rest. (You can skip *all* of it, if you like; Facebook doesn't require you to fill out any profile information.) Here's how to add basic info to your profile:

1. **At the top of any Facebook screen, click the "edit" link.**

2. **On the page that appears, click the Basic tab (if it's not already selected).**

3. **In the Basic window, fill in as many of the following fields as you like:**

- **Sex.** From the drop-down list, choose Male or Female.

- **Birthday.** If you accidentally gave Facebook the wrong date when you signed up, you can change the day or month of your birth here (but not the year). To hide your age or birthday from folks who can see your profile, from the "in my profile" drop-down list choose "Show only month & day" or "Don't show my birthday".

**Tip** If your fingers slipped during the registration and you need to change your birth year, you can't do that on the Basic tab. You have to request the change from Facebook's customer service (*www.facebook.com/cs_forms/birthday.php*).

| | |
|---|---|
| Basic Contact Relationships Personal Education Work Picture Layout | |
| Sex: | Select Sex: ▾ |
| Birthday: | Jan ▾ 26 ▾ 1937 |
| | Show my full birthday ▾ in my profile. |
| Hometown: | |
| Country: | Select Country: ▾ |
| Political Views: | Select Political Views: ▾ |
| Religious Views: | |
| | Save Changes Cancel |

- **Hometown.** Type in any city you like; Facebook doesn't match this name against the country, state, or province you select.

- **Country.** When you choose the country you live in from the drop-down list, Facebook displays additional fields, such as state (if you choose United States) or province (if you choose Canada).

- **Political views.** Cast your vote for Liberal, Conservative, or another label from this drop-down list.

- **Religious Views.** Type whatever you like in this field. If you need more than the 100 characters Facebook gives you, you can expound on your theological leanings in the About Me field of the Personal section (page 12).

4. **When you're finished, click Save Changes.** Or, if you want to discard what you entered, click Cancel.

## Adding Contact Information

After you register, Facebook members can contact you several different ways, including sending you a message in Facebook and writing on your Facebook "wall." But if you like, you can give folks additional ways to contact you by listing your street address, phone number, and instant messaging screen names. Here's how:

1. **At the top of any Facebook screen, click the "edit" link, and then click the Contact tab.**

Basic  Contact  Relationships  Personal  Education  Work  Picture  Layout

| | | |
|---|---|---|
| **Emails:** | eamoore68@gmail.com<br>Add / Remove Emails | 🔒 Only my friends |
| **Screen Name(s):** | [　　　　　　　]  AIM ▼ | |
| | Add another screen name | 🔒 Only my friends |
| **Mobile Phone:** | [　　　　　　　] | 🔒 Only my friends |
| **Land Phone:** | [　　　　　　　] | 🔒 Only my friends |
| **Address:** | [　　　　　　　] | |
| **City:** | [　　　　　　　] | |
| **Country:** | Select Country: ▼ | |
| **Zip:** | [　　　　　　　] | 🔒 Only my friends |
| **Website:** | [　　　　　　　] | |
| | | 🔒 Only my friends |

Save Changes    Cancel

2. **In the Contact window that appears, fill in as many of the following fields as you like:**

> **Note** Clicking the "Only my friends" lock icon next to a field tells Facebook to hide the contents of that field from anyone you haven't specifically accepted as a Facebook friend. For example, by clicking the icon next to Mobile Phone, you can make it so that Sarah (who's in your network) *can't* see your cellphone number when she pulls up your Facebook profile, but George (who's one of your Facebook friends) *can*. See Chapter 13 for details.

- **Emails.** Oddly, clicking Add/Remove Emails doesn't actually let you add or remove emails. Instead, clicking this link lets you change your primary email address—the one you entered when signing up for your Facebook account (page 2).

> **Note** Although Facebook restricts you to a single *primary* email address, you can associate multiple email addresses with your account, which is useful if you want to join multiple networks. For the how-to, see page 30.

- **Screen Name(s).** If you've already got an account with an instant messaging service such as AIM (AOL Instant Messenger), you can add your instant messaging alias or *screen name* to your account. Doing so lets anybody looking at your Facebook profile see if you're logged into your instant messaging program (Facebook displays a green dot next to your screen name when you're logged in). If you're logged in, people with an instant messaging program installed on their computers can click your screen name to start messaging you.

  To add a screen name, type it into the field and then, from the drop-down list, select your instant messaging service. Your choices are AIM, Google Talk, Skype, Windows Live, Yahoo, Gadu-Gadu, and ICQ. Facebook lets you add up to five different screen names.

- **Mobile Phone, Land Phone, Address, City, Country, Zip.** If you wouldn't feel comfortable heading to your local community center and tacking up a flyer listing your phone number and street address, you probably don't want to add these details to your Facebook profile.

- **Website.** You can list multiple Web sites; just make sure you type each URL (such as *www.mycoolsite.com*) on its own line. Feel free to skip the *http://*; Facebook adds it automatically.

3. **When you're finished, click Save Changes, or click Cancel to discard your changes.**

## Adding Personal Information

Thanks to its roots as a souped-up yearbook for college students, Facebook encourages you to wax rhapsodic about such personal details as your hobbies, your favorite bands, and what you're looking for in a potential mate. To add that kind of info, follow these steps:

1. **At the top of any Facebook screen, click the "edit" link, and then click the Personal tab.**

2. **In the Personal window that appears, type as much as you like into any of the fields: Activities, Interests, Favorite Music, Favorite TV Shows, Favorite Movies, Favorite Books, Favorite Quotes, and About Me.**

**Tip** Adding reams of personal tidbits—for example, typing a couple pages' worth of info into every field in the Personal tab—marks you as a Facebook newbie.

3. **When you finish, click Save Changes and Facebook automatically updates your profile.** (Click Cancel to discard your changes.)

**Tip** Unless you plan to use Facebook as an online dating service, you can probably skip the next three steps.

4. **Click the Relationships tab.**

5. **Turn on the checkboxes and select from the drop-down list to describe your relationship status and preferences.**

| Basic  Contact  Relationships  Personal  Education  Work  Picture  Layout |
|---|

| | |
|---|---|
| Interested in: | ☐ Men  ☐ Women |
| Relationship Status: | Select Status: ▼ |
| Looking for: | ☐ Friendship  ☐ Dating |
| | ☐ A Relationship  ☐ Random play |
| | ☐ Whatever I can get |
| | Save Changes  Cancel |

6. **When you're done, click Save Changes or Cancel.**

# Adding Academic and Work-related Information

If you're a student or work at a decent-sized company, adding a few school- or work-related details to your profile is well worth your time. After all, the whole point of Facebook is to try to mimic your real social circles—and if you're like most folks, a lot of your real-life friends are fellow students and co-workers.

Taking the time to add these details also comes in handy for connecting with long-lost pals, because Facebook lets you search for people based on matching profile details. So, for example, you can easily look up folks who were in your graduating class.

To add details about the schools you attend now (or attended in the past):

1. **At the top of any Facebook screen, click the "edit" link, and then click the Education tab.**

2. **In the Education window that appears, fill out any of the following optional fields:**

- **College/University.** As soon as you start typing, Facebook pops up a helpful list of schools you can choose from. You can add up to five different colleges or universities.

- **Class Year.** Choose your graduation year from the drop-down list.

- **Attended for.** Your choices are College or Graduate School.

- **Concentration.** Type in the subject you majored (or minored) in. If you double majored in school, click "Add another concentration" to add up to three different subjects.

- **High School.** Facebook lets you list up to two different high schools.

- **Class Year.** Choose the year you graduated high school from the drop-down list.

**Tip** The email address you used to sign up for your Facebook account doesn't have to be a valid school email address (one that ends in .edu, such as me@myschool.edu) for you to add school details.

3. **Click Save Changes or Cancel.**

To add details about your work life:

1. **At the top of any Facebook screen, click the "edit" link, and then click the Work tab.**

2. **In the Work window that appears, fill out any of the following fields:**

- **Employer.** As soon as you start typing, Facebook pops up the list of companies it knows about. If the company you work for is among them, select it from the list; if not, just type in the name.

Basic  Contact  Relationships  Personal  Education  Work  Picture  Layout

Employer:
(required)

Position:

Description:

City/Town:

Time Period:  ☑ I currently work here.

Month: ▼  Year: ▼ to present.

Add another job...

Save Changes    Cancel

- **Position, Description, City/Town.**
- **Time Period.** Turn on this checkbox if you're still at this job, and then click to select the month and year you started. If you leave this checkbox turned off, Facebook displays another set of Month/Year fields for the date you left the company.

**Note** You can list up to five different employers/jobs by clicking the "Add another job" link.

# Adding Pictures of Yourself

Until you add a picture to your profile, Facebook displays a giant question mark. Replacing that question mark with a picture of yourself is a good idea because it helps searchers identify you more easily. But you don't have to stop with a single profile picture. Facebook lets you create a Profile Picture Album containing multiple pictures, each of which you can give an optional caption (see page 18).

Facebook lets you upload additional photo albums (page 163) and even *tag* the pictures you upload—including your profile picture. *Tagging* is a nifty way of assigning a portion of a picture to a specific Facebook member's name. For example, say you upload a shot of yourself that shows a co-worker lurking in the background. You can drag your mouse to outline your own head and assign that portion of the picture to your own name, and then outline your co-worker and assign that portion of the picture to your co-worker's name. Tagging helps Facebook members find pictures that include them, wherever those pictures may appear—on a friend's site or a mortal enemy's. For the skinny on tagging, check out page 170.

1. **At the top of any Facebook screen, click the "edit" link, and then click the Picture tab.**

Basic Contact Relationships Personal Education Work Picture Layout

**Current Picture**

**Upload Picture**

You can upload a JPG, GIF or PNG file.

[                              ] [ Browse... ]

☐ I certify that I have the right to distribute this picture and that it does not violate the Terms of Use.

[ Upload Picture ]

File size limit 4 MB. If your upload does not work, try a smaller picture.

2. **In the Picture window that appears, click Browse.** The File Upload window that appears lets you search your computer for the picture file you want to add. Make sure the file you choose has an extension of .jpg, .gif, or .png, and that it's smaller than 4 megabytes (it probably is—JPG, GIF, and PNG files tend to be pretty small). After you make your selection, the name of your file appears in the Upload Picture field.

3. **Turn on the "I certify" checkbox.** You can click the Terms of Use link to read the legal nitty-gritty of what you're agreeing to, but here's the bottom line: Don't add a picture that you didn't personally shoot (or draw, or airbrush, or whatever).

4. **Click Upload Picture.** The next time you view your profile (page 7), you see your picture instead of the giant question mark.

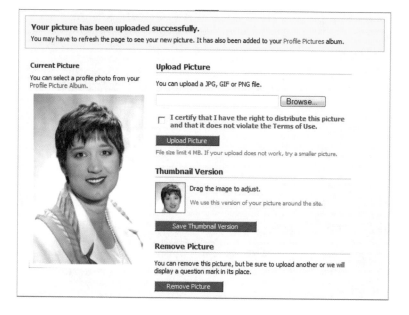

**Your picture has been uploaded successfully.**
You may have to refresh the page to see your new picture. It has also been added to your Profile Pictures album.

**Current Picture**
You can select a profile photo from your Profile Picture Album.

**Upload Picture**
You can upload a JPG, GIF or PNG file.

Browse...

☐ I certify that I have the right to distribute this picture and that it does not violate the Terms of Use.

Upload Picture

File size limit 4 MB. If your upload does not work, try a smaller picture.

**Thumbnail Version**

Drag the image to adjust.
We use this version of your picture around the site.

Save Thumbnail Version

**Remove Picture**
You can remove this picture, but be sure to upload another or we will display a question mark in its place.

Remove Picture

5. **If you like, you can tweak your picture or add more pictures to create a Profile Picture Album.** Here are your options:

- **To upload an additional picture** to your Profile Picture Album, simply repeat steps 2–4.

- **To change your profile picture to another picture you've already added,** click the Profile Picture Album link (it's on the left, above your current picture). Then, in the window that appears, click the picture you want. Finally, at the bottom of the window (scroll way down), click the Make Profile Picture link and, in the confirmation box that appears, click the Yep! button.

  Facebook displays a tiny thumbnail version of your profile picture in various places around the site depending on your Facebook activities. For example, if you join a group (Chapter 6), Facebook displays your thumbnail on the Members section of the group's profile page. If you become friends with another member, your thumbnail appears on that person's Friend List.

- **To tweak the thumbnail version of your profile picture**, mouse over the thumbnail until your cursor turns into a four-headed arrow; then drag to move the contents of the picture around in its teensy-tiny thumbnail frame. When you're happy with the way things look, click Save Thumbnail Version.

- **To delete a picture from your Profile Picture Album**, click the Profile Picture Album link, click the picture you want to remove, and then click Delete This Photo.

- Captions appear when folks viewing your photo album mouse over pictures. **To add a caption to your profile picture**, click the Profile Picture Album link, and then click Edit Photos. In the window that appears, head to the Caption field that's next to your profile picture, type your caption text, and then click Save Changes.

> **Tip** For a site that doesn't advertise itself as a photo-sharing site, Facebook lets you do a surprising amount of stuff to your pictures. You can create multiple photo albums, order prints online, share your photos with Facebook members (and non-Facebook members)—even rotate your photos 90 degrees. At the top of any Facebook screen, click the "edit" link, click the Picture tab, and then click the Profile Picture Album link. In the My Photos—Profile Pictures window that appears, click any picture, and then scroll to the bottom of the window to see your options.

# Viewing Your Facebook Home Page

After you've registered with Facebook, Facebook creates a home page just for you. To see it:

1. **In your Web browser, go to www.facebook.com.** You see a generic welcome page with a spot for you to log in to Facebook on the left.

2. **Log in.** If you always access Facebook from the same computer, you may find your email address already appears in the Email field. If not, type in the email address and password you gave Facebook when you registered, and then click the Login button.

3. **After you finish your Facebook session, click the "logout" link in the upper-right part of any Facebook screen.** Doing so prevents other folks from getting into your profile and designating you as looking for "Whatever I can get".

# Changing Account Information

Some of the information you share with Facebook—like your password and, optionally, your credit card number, for example—isn't for public consumption. Because these details are between you and Facebook, they're not part of your profile, but are part of your Facebook account.

To change your account details:

1. **At the top of any Facebook screen, click the "account" link.**

2. **In the window that appears, make sure the Settings tab is selected.**

3. **Click the link next to one or more of the following fields:**

- **Name.** If your name changes after you register with Facebook—due to a marriage or divorce, for example—you can update it instead of canceling your membership and re-registering. One caveat: Because Facebook runs your name change through security checks to spot potential fraud, your name change won't take effect immediately. (Think days, not hours.)

- **Contact Email.** If your email address changes, you need to let Facebook know.

**Tip** Depending on how much you use Facebook, your email inbox might be swamped with emails telling you to log in to Facebook and check your Facebook messages. If this happens to you, consider getting a new email address just for your Facebook account. You can get a free email address from sites like *www.yahoo.com* or *www.google.com*.

- **Password.** For security reasons, you have to type in your old password, and then type in your new password twice.

- **Credit Cards.** You don't need to bother filling in your credit card information until you're ready to pay Facebook for a gift (page 71) or some form of advertising (page 177).

- **Deactivate Account.** If you don't like Facebook, you can just stop using it, but Facebook gives you a better way to break things off. By deactivating your account, you get a chance to tell Facebook's designers why you don't like it (actually, you can't deactivate until you *do*). And turning on the "Opt out of receiving emails from Facebook." checkbox during the deactivation process lets you stop Facebook-related notifications and invitations from appearing in your inbox.

# Joining a Network

What Facebook does best is track connections between people who've joined the site. The easiest way to make a bunch of Facebook connections in one fell swoop is to join a *network*—a group of people who have something in common: graduates and current attendees of a particular school, fellow employees at a company, residents of a town, and so on. Joining a network takes a lot of the grunt work out of finding interesting real-world groups and events, shopping for local stuff, and contacting real-life friends and co-workers. You can't just join any ol' network, though—there are some restrictions, as this chapter explains. And if you want to *create* a new network, you can suggest it to Facebook. Read on for the full scoop.

# How Networks Work

A Facebook *network* is simply a group of people who live, work, or go to school in the same place. You'll probably want to join at least one network as soon as you register, because until you do, the only folks whose profiles you can see are those you specifically tell Facebook you want to be friends with (see Chapter 3), and the only events and groups you can see are "global" ones—which is about as exciting as reading through the *New York Times* want ads when you live in L.A.

**Note** You can't see a network member's profile until you join that network, but you *can* see a few public details, such as the member's profile pictures and friends.

When you join a network, two things happen:

- **You get immediate access to the Facebook profiles of all fellow network members, as well as access to the network's groups, events, market listings, and other goodies.** There are a few exceptions. Some Facebook members choose to hide their profiles, and some groups and events are restricted, too (see Chapter 13). But you still get access to a mountain of dishy details—all of which are potentially useful and interesting to you, because you have something big in common with all the other network members: the city you live in, the school you go to, or the company you work for.

**Note** After you've joined a network or two, you can home in on people who share a common interest (such as Oprah fans, marathon runners, or needle felters) by creating or joining a Facebook *group*. See Chapter 6 for the skinny on groups.

**Posted Items**    See All

We have since found a car seat that was held a child up in a PC crash a few more harness makes the BRAKE RECENT

Importance of a 5-Point Harness Carseat
http://www.youtube.com/watch?v=azgBhZfcqaQ

BlackNailsPaintedOff6264's music tastes
http://fb-share.ilike.com/user/BlackNailsPaintedO...

MySpaceTV: When men get horny.. by Chris Crocker
http://www.myspacetv.com/index.cfm?fuseaction=vid...

Importance of a 5-Point Harness Carseat

**Groups**    See All

THE | LIMITE DE LOS
ES. | ESTADOS UNIDOS
MEXICANOS
CONTIGO INTERNACIONAL
DE LIMITE A AAAAA

Mcallen-ers Around the Globe
207 members (208 new)

El Derek's man club
140 members (31 new)

Mcallen-ers Around the Globe

I don't whisper, I text.
140 members (141 new)

**Discussion Board**

Displaying 3 of 12 discussion topics.    Start New Topic | See All

**friends needed!!!!!**
4 posts by 4 people. Updated 48 minutes ago.

**myRGVsports.com**
2 posts by 1 person. Updated on Sep 29, 2007 at 10:39 AM.

**WOW!!Explosive news, HDQR.net is USA Biggest sell Games CD-KEY website (www.hdqr.net)**
1 post by 1 person. Updated on Sep 29, 2007 at 3:12 AM.

The Wall

**Marketplace**

List Something    See All

Korn/Hellyeah/5fingerdeat;
Have 1 ticket for the Korn con...

Spanish Tutor
I'd like to hire a Spanis...

Record Player Repairman
I have an old
Montgomery Ward ...

**Network Statistics**

**Top TV**

1  Family Guy
2  Csi
3  Lost
4  Grey's Anatomy
5  Friends
6  Smallville
7  Desperate Housewives
8  Scrubs
9  Futurama
10 Seinfeld

See more stats »

**Nearby Networks**

- **Everybody else in the network can look up your profile information—including a running list of all the things you've been doing
in Facebook.** Network members can also see your hometown, your
political views, your contact email address, and everything else you
added to your profile. And by viewing the *mini-feed* (a running list of
your activities on Facebook) that automatically shows up on your profile, they can also see that an hour ago you uploaded a picture, half
an hour ago you joined a group, and two minutes ago you received a
gift.

**Tip**  It's one thing to let everyone in your network see the details you specifically added
to your profile; it's another to let them peek over your virtual shoulder as you go
about your business in Facebook. Seriously, do you really want the whole world to
know that you changed your religious views 12 times in the last two hours or left
your online knitting group in a huff? To learn how to keep network members you
haven't specifically "friended" from being able to view your mini-feed see page 230.

# Viewing the Networks You're Already On

Maybe you've already joined a network. (You may have, depending on the selection you chose from the "I am" drop-down list when you registered for Facebook; see page 3.) Maybe you can't remember if you have or you haven't. To see which networks you've already joined, do one of the following:

- **At the top of any Facebook screen, click the down arrow next to Networks to see a list of the networks you're in.**

| Networks ▾ | Inbox |
| --- | --- |
| O'Reilly Media | |
| Harvard | |
| New York, NY | |
| | |
| Browse All Networks | |
| Join a Network | |

- **At the top of any Facebook screen, click Networks to see a tabbed page for each of the networks you're in.**

| O'Reilly Media | Harvard | New York, NY |
| --- | --- | --- |

**New York, NY**                                    Browse other Networks

**Network Info**                    **People in New York, NY**

Members:    612,785              Displaying 6 of 612,785 people.          Search | Browse
Friends:    4
Type:       Regional

Browse All Networks
See What's Popular              Ahmed                    Alex              Andrew S.   Karim
View Discussion Board           Saleh    Peter Parker  Epelboym  Kate Kataja   Tosi      Gaye

**Upcoming Events**
Displaying 5 of 55 events occurring today.                                      See All

Dec 17    2008 Sprint Triathaolon  @ Port Washington          December 2007
          Today from 9:35 am to 12:35 pm          Sun Mon Tue Wed Thu Fri Sat
                                                                              1
          Good Luck on Finals!  @ Queens College
          Today at 11:00 am until Fri Dec 21 at 2:00 pm – (20     2   3   4   5   6   7   8
          attendees)
                                                                9  10  11  12  13  14  15
          AT NIGHT with GABE AND JENNY  @ RIFIFI
          Today from 1:00 pm to 4:00 pm

**Note:** Facebook automatically adds the *Global network* (see the next section for info on that unexclusive club) to everybody's account, but it doesn't appear in your list or in its own tabbed page. You see the Global network only when you go to join a group or event.

# Joining a Network

When you register, Facebook automatically assigns you to the not-super-useful Global network, which gives you access to globally organized groups and events. But you definitely want to join at least one more network. Technically, you can belong to as many as five different networks, but if you're like most people, two or three (a regional network plus a network for your work, school, or both) fills the bill. Anyone can join a regional network (like the one for Denver, CO, for example), but you have to have a company-issued email address to join a company's network, and a school-issued email address to join a school's network.

> **Note** For security reasons, you can't join multiple regional networks (meaning, you can't tell Facebook you live both in Phoenix and Miami) and you can't switch networks every two minutes, either. In fact, Facebook limits you to two changes per network per two-month period—and if you actually change that often, your account may be flagged by Facebook's fraud-sniffers. So when you choose a network, make sure it's the one you really want.

To join a network:

1. **At the top of any Facebook screen, click the down arrow next to Networks.**

2. **In the drop-down list that appears, click "Join a Network".**

> **Note** You can't just join any old network—you have to have a valid email address that matches the workplace, college, or high school network you want to join. For example, if your email address is *frank_furter@ibm.com*, Facebook lets you join the IBM workplace network. If your email address is *guy_wire@asu.edu*, Facebook lets you join the Arizona State University college network.
>
> Fortunately, you're not limited to one email address (and therefore one network). You can join multiple networks as long as you have multiple valid email addresses — for example, an email address from the school where you picked up your undergrad degree, one from the school where you transferred to get your master's, and one from your employer. To join additional networks, follow the steps in this section, once through for each email address you have.

3. **Click one of the following links based on the type of network you want to join:**

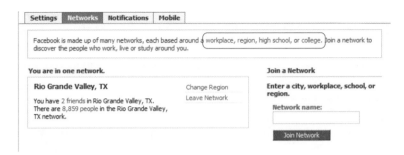

- **Workplace.** After you click the "workplace" link, you see the Workplaces page showing a list of companies that Facebook knows about. Click through the alphabet to find your company, and then click its link. Finally, in the confirmation box that appears, click the Join This Network link. If the email you used to register for Facebook matches the company you chose, you're in; if not, Facebook displays an error message.

**Browse All Networks**

Facebook is made up of many networks, each based around a workplace, region, high school or college.

**Search for a Network:**

Enter a city, workplace, school, or region.

| Regions | Colleges | **Workplaces** | High Schools |
|---------|----------|------------|--------------|

**A** B C D E F G H I J K L M N O P Q R S T U V W X Y Z

**Available Workplaces**

| | | |
|---|---|---|
| A & A Global Industries | Alexander Technologies | Answer Financial |
| A & A Portables | Alexandria Clinic | Antelope Valley Hospital |
| A & B TV | Alfa Flower Shop | Antelope Valley Nissan |
| A & D Automatic Gate | Alfred Angelo | Anteon |
| A & E Stores | Alfred Benesch & Co | Anthony & Sylvan Pools |
| A & K Earth Movers | Alfred Conhagen | Anthony Forest Products |
| A & K Energy Conservation | Alfred Heller | Anthony Mechanical Services |
| A & L Underground | Alfred Matthews | Anthropologie |
| A & M Supply | Alfred Nickles Bakery | Antibus Scales & Systems |

**Note** If you don't see your company listed, you can ask Facebook to add it to its network list (see page 30).

- **Region.** After you click the "region" link, the Regions page appears. Start typing the name of your city (or county, or area) into the "Search for a Network" box in the upper right, and choose from the drop-down list that appears as you type. On the network page that appears, click the Join This Network link. Unlike workplace- and school-related networks, you don't need any particular email address to join a regional network.

> **Note** Facebook lets you join only one regional network at a time. If you try to add a second, Facebook simply replaces the first with the second. That's kind of annoying if you're a multiple-home owner, but on the bright side, you own multiple homes.

**Browse All Networks**

Facebook is made up of many networks, each based around a workplace, region, high school or college.

**Search for a Network:**

Enter a city, workplace, school, or region.

| Regions | Colleges | Workplaces | High Schools |

Jump to Canada | Jump to Great Britain | Jump to Regions Elsewhere

**Available Regions in the USA**

| **Alabama** | **Maine** | **Oregon** |
|---|---|---|
| Birmingham, AL | Auburn / Lewiston, ME | Bend, OR |
| Dothan, AL | Bangor, ME | Corvallis, OR |
| Huntsville / Decatur, AL | Portland, ME | Eugene, OR |
| Mobile, AL | **Maryland** | Medford, OR |
| Montgomery, AL | Baltimore, MD | Portland, OR |
| **Alaska** | Salisbury, MD | Salem, OR |
| Anchorage, AK | **Massachusetts** | **Pennsylvania** |
| Central Alaska, AK | Boston, MA | Allentown, PA |
| Juneau, AK | Cape Cod, MA | Erie, PA |
| **Arizona** | Lowell, MA | Harrisburg, PA |
| Northern Arizona, AZ | Springfield, MA | Lancaster, PA |

- **High school.** High school networks don't work the same as other Facebook networks. Specifically, you can't add a high school network. Instead, when you register for Facebook—using either a valid high school email address or by responding to an invitation from a Facebook member who goes to your high school—Facebook automatically plops you in the correct high school network. If you're not using a valid high school email address, you have to be confirmed by a handful of friends—other Facebook network members who can vouch that they know you and that you attend the high school that matches your email address—before Facebook will let you in. You can only switch high school networks once every six months.

- **College.** After you click the "college" link, the Colleges page appears. Click the drop-down list to choose your state or country, and then—from the list that appears—choose a college.

> **Note** If you've already graduated, no sweat: Alumni email addresses work, too. If you don't have one, contact your college to see if you can wrangle one.

**Browse All Networks**

Facebook is made up of many networks, each based around a workplace, region, high school or college.

**Search for a Network:**

Enter a city, workplace, school, or

| Regions | Colleges | Workplaces | High Schools |

Select Region: Alaska ▼

**Available Colleges**

| Alaska Anch | Alaska Fair | Alaska Southeast |
| Alaska Bible | Alaska Pacific | Sheldon Jackson |

4. **If you like, join additional networks (you can join up to five total).** To do so: At the top of any Facebook screen, click the down arrow next to Networks and, in the drop-down list that appears, click "Join a Network". On the Networks page, in the "Network name" field, start typing the region, workplace, or school network you want to join. As soon as Facebook displays the name of the network you're looking for, click it. Facebook displays additional fields you need to fill out, including a new email address. (For example, if you're an alumnus and want to join your old school's network, Facebook asks you for a valid school email address.) When you finish filling out all the fields, click the Join Network button.

# Suggesting a New Network

Maybe you work for a small company or live in a tiny backwater town. If you check Facebook's network listings and don't see a network that describes where you go to school, live, or work, you can ask Facebook to add your school, region, or company to its network listings. Just follow these steps:

1. **At the top of any Facebook screen, click the down arrow next to Networks.**

2. **From the drop-down list, choose Browse All Networks.**

3. **On the page that appears, make sure the Regions tab is selected.** If it's not, click to select it.

4. **Scroll to the bottom of the page and click "Suggest a new network".**

| Federated States of Micronesia | Nicaragua | Western Sahara |
| Fiji | Niger | Yemen |
| Finland | Nigeria | Zambia |
| France | North Korea | Zimbabwe |
| French Guiana | Northern Ireland | |
| French Polynesia | Northern Mariana Islands | |

Is your network not supported? Suggest a new network.

5. **Choose a network type (High School, College, Work, or Region) from the drop-down list and fill out the fields that appear.**

| Suggestions | Safety |

If you have a problem with your account, please go to the Help section.

**Suggest a New Network**

Facebook is comprised of networks corresponding to colleges, high schools, workplaces, and geographic regions. If you would like us to add a network for a school, workplace or region we're missing, indicate the type of network you're requesting and provide the details below:

**Network Type:** Region

**Region Name:**
High School
College
**Country:** Work
Region

**City:**

**Your Contact Email:** (optional)

(We'll contact you at this address when we add your network.)

Submit

6. **When you're done, click Submit.** Because actual people need to approve your request, expect to wait a few days or even weeks for Facebook to get back to you. (There's no guarantee they'll approve your request, but if your network suggestion is reasonable, you'll probably get a thumbs-up.)

# Finding and Adding Friends

In real life, your social network consists not just of people who live in your town and work or study where you do, but also of people you've formed one-on-one relationships with: teachers, ex-sisters-in-law, bowling buddies, and so on. It's the same with Facebook: You start with a network of school or work buddies (see Chapter 2), and then add friends one at a time. You can even use Facebook to look up old friends and find new ones.

Why would you want to enlarge your Facebook social circle? Well, having friends is really the whole point of joining Facebook. You get to swap life-in-progress tidbits (both serious and silly), share what you're reading, play online games...the list is endless. But first you need to gather your pals. Read on to learn how.

# How Facebook Friends Work

In the world of Facebook, a *friend* is any Facebook member who has agreed that you two have something in common. Maybe you play on the same softball team, volunteer at the local animal shelter together, or keep running into each other at parties thrown by the same ex-roommate. Maybe you dated, took a road trip together, or you're second cousins twice removed. How you know a Facebook friend doesn't matter; all that matters is that you *both* agree that you know each other.

> **Note** Facebook has no way of verifying the relationships between friends. But one of the major differences between Facebook and *MySpace.com*—the other big social networking site—is that Facebook strongly encourages truthfulness. So, while having a zillion "friends" is considered a status symbol on MySpace, it's not on Facebook. On Facebook, the goal of friends is to put together a manageable list of people you actually know—and actually care about keeping up with.

Two people become Facebook friends when one person extends an invitation and the other person accepts, or *confirms.* When you become friends with someone in Facebook, three things happen:

- **You appear on your friend's *Friend List* (page 50) and on her profile page (and vice versa).** On Facebook, as in life, you're known by the company you keep: Everyone with access to your friend's profile (or yours) can see the relationship between the two of you. And with the click of a mouse, folks can hop from your friend's profile to yours, or from your profile to your friend's.

> **Note** One of the best, most addictive things about Facebook is its confessional nature. Facebook *profiles* encourage members to pontificate at length about subjects that don't often come up in polite conversation. So, when you're friends with someone in Facebook, you might be surprised at the juicy details you learn about them.

- **You can see your friend's profile (and vice versa) even if he's not in your network.** This means you can see the events he's planning to attend, the groups he's joined, and all the other people he's friends with, among other personal details.

- **You can sign up to receive automatic detail-packed updates, such as** *news feeds* **(page 78), chronicling your friend's Facebook activities (and vice versa).**

**October 12**

Patsy Alvarado **added new photos to a group.**

Mothers of Brownsville (MOB)
4 photos

Charity Avendano **activated** Facebook Mobile.

Patsy Alvarado and Emily Vlasich Lefler are now friends.

**Note** Chapter 5 shows you how to sign up for updates on your friends' Facebook activities—including news feeds—and how to customize the updates your friends get about you.

# Finding Friends

Before you can make someone your friend, you first have to find that person on Facebook. The site gives you three different ways to do this:

- You can look up real-life friends and acquaintances who are already Facebook members.

- You can invite real-life friends and acquaintances who aren't on Facebook yet to join the site.

- You can search for Facebook members you've never met but who share your interests (such as a background in server-side technology or a passion for container gardening).

## Finding People Who Are Facebook Members

Some of your real-life friends and acquaintances might already be Facebook members. To find them, use one of the following search methods:

- **Search for Facebook members by name.** In the Search field on the left side of any Facebook screen, type the name of the person you're looking for and hit Return. Facebook displays all the matches (and near-matches) it finds in all networks. If you see a ton of matches, click the People tab so your list won't be cluttered with groups or events that happen to match your search criteria. To narrow your search to a single network, choose a network from the "Show results from" drop-down list. To narrow it down by sex, age, or relationship status, click the blue Show More Filters link.

> **Tip** In Facebook, clickable links are blue. If one of the names you see in the search results (or on your friends list, or anywhere else in Facebook) is blue, then clicking it takes you straight to that person's profile.

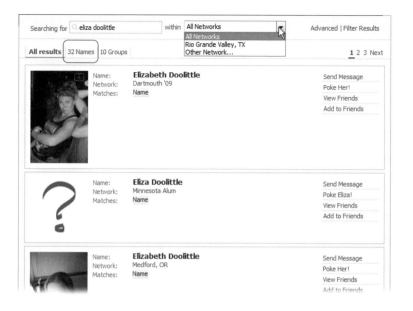

- **Search for Facebook members who are classmates, ex-classmates, or co-workers.** On the left side of any Facebook screen, click the down arrow next to the word Search and choose Find Classmates or Find Coworkers. In the fields that appear, type in either the name of the school and graduating year of the class you're looking for, or the name of a company. Then type in the name of the person you're looking for and click "Search for".

**Search by High School**

High School: [                    ]   Class Year: [  ▾  ]
Person's Name: [                    ]
(optional)

[ Search for Classmates ]


**Search by College**

College: [ ASU              ]   Class Year: [  ▾  ]
Person's Name: [                    ]
(optional)

[ Search for Classmates ]


**Search by Company**

Company: [                    ]
Person's Name: [                    ]
(optional)

[ Search for Coworkers ]


- **Search for people you regularly email from your Web-based email account.** If you have a Web-based email address (such as *your_name@ gmail.com* or *your_name@yahoo.com*), you can give Facebook your email password and let it scan your email address book for matching Facebook members.


| Friend List | **Find Friends** | Status Updates | Social Timeline |

**Are Your Friends Already on Facebook?**

📧 **Web Email** Yahoo Mail, Hotmail, Gmail, etc.
Find out which of your email contacts are on Facebook.

Your Email: [ eamoore68        ] @ [ gmail.com   ▾ ]

Email Password: [                    ]

[ Find Your Friends ]

We won't store your login or password or email anyone without
your permission.

[ 🔵 **AIM Instant Messenger** ] Find your AIM buddies on Facebook
[ 📇 **Email Application** ] Outlook, Apple Mail, etc.

More Ways to Find Friends »

Here's how: At the top of any Facebook screen, click the down arrow next to Friends, and then click Find Friends to display the Find Friends tab. If the email address Facebook suggests on the Find Friends tab is correct, type in your email password. If not, type in your email ID (the part of your email address before the @ symbol) and, from the drop-down list, choose your email provider—and *then* type in your email password. When you finish, click Find Your Friends. If Facebook finds members who match the email addresses in your Web-based email address book, it displays them; if it doesn't find any matches, it pops up a message box asking if you'd like to try a different Web email account.

**Note** You don't have to have registered for Facebook with a Web email account to use this search method. For example, if you registered for Facebook with your work email address (like me@mycompany.com), you can still search your Gmail address book.

| Friend List | **Find Friends** | Status Updates | Social Timeline |

**Are Your Friends Already on Facebook?**

**Web Email** Yahoo Mail, Hotmail, Gmail, etc.
Find out which of your email contacts are on Facebook.

Your Email:  `sarah_bellum`  @ `msn.com` ▼

Email Password:  `••••••••••`

[ Find Your Friends ]

We won't store your login or password or email anyone without your permission.

**Note** Keep in mind that when you enter your email account password you're handing over some pretty sensitive info to Facebook. After all, that password's the virtual key to your email, your address book, and probably a bunch of other personal goodies. While Facebook is a reputable outfit and pledges not to store your info, you might want to skip this step if this whole sharing business makes you queasy.

- **Search for people you regularly instant message.** If you use AOL Instant Messenger (AIM), you can give Facebook your AIM screen name and password and let it scan your buddy list for matching Facebook members. To do so: On the Find Friends tab (at the top of any screen, click the down arrow next to Friends, and then choose Find Friends), click AIM Instant Messenger to display the Screen Name and AIM Password fields. Enter your screen name and password, and then click Find Friends. Facebook either displays matching Facebook members, or pops up a message box asking if you'd like to try your search again (you don't; if Facebook didn't find any matches the first time, it won't find any matches the second).

AIM Instant Messenger Find your AIM buddies on Facebook
Find out which of your AIM Buddies are on Facebook.

Screen Name: spidey
AIM Password: •••••••••

Find Friends

We won't store your login info or contact anyone without your permission.

- **Search for people you regularly email, using a list of contacts.** Depending on the email program you use, you can export a list of email addresses from your email program and let Facebook scan the addresses for matching Facebook members. (If you use a Web-based email account, see page 38.) To do so: Create a *contact file*, a list of email addresses separated by tabs or commas. (If you need help doing this, on the Find Friends tab [at the top of any screen, click the down arrow next to Friends, and then choose Find Friends], click Email Application to display the Contact File field, and then click the "how to create a contact file here" link. Click the link for your particular email program and follow the instructions for creating a contact file.) Then give Facebook the name of the contact file you just created. Click Browse to select the contact file. After you do, Facebook either displays the Facebook members who match your email list, or shows you a link you can use to get technical help.

**Email Application** Outlook, Apple Mail, etc.

Upload a contact file and we will tell you which of your contacts are on Facebook.
Read how to create a contact file here.

Outlook

Outlook Express

Windows Address Book

Thunderbird

Palm Desktop

Palm Desktop (vCard)

Entourage

Mac OS X Address Book

Other

Still having problems? Contact us.

**Contact File:** [                    ] [ Browse... ]

# Finding People Who Aren't Facebook Members

You can't add people to your Friend List unless they're Facebook members. But say you've got a few real-life pals you wish would sign up for the site so you could keep in touch more easily. Facebook gives you an easy way to invite these people to join:

1. **At the top of any Facebook screen, click the down arrow next to Friends, and then click Invite Friends.**

2. **On the Invite Your Friends page that appears, type in your non-Facebook-pals' email addresses, separated by commas; then type in a quick message and click Invite.** Facebook sends invitations to all the addresses in the To field.

**Invite Your Friends**

From: Emily Moore <eamoore68@gmail.com>

To: guy_wire@hotmail.com, ben_dover@gmail.com,
(use commas to separate emails) eileen_dover@yahoo.mail

**Import Email Addresses** ▸
from your Yahoo, Hotmail, AOL, Gmail or MSN address book.

Hotmail  Gmail
YAHOO! Mail  AOL

Message: You gotta check out Facebook!
(optional)

[ Invite ]  [ Cancel ]

**Tip** If you have more than a handful of email addresses to type in, consider having Facebook grab them from your Web email account (page 38) or from a file you export from your email program (page 40).

## Finding New Friends

One of the reasons Facebook is so popular is that it lets you connect with kindred spirits. Want to meet other people who like your favorite TV shows, live in your town, or share your political views? Easy. And because Facebook wisely limits in-depth searching to fellow members of the networks you've joined, you already have something in common with the people you look up in Facebook: where you live, where you work, or where you go (or went) to school. Voilà—instant conversation opener!

To search for other Facebook members based on profile details:

1. **On the left side of any Facebook screen, click the down arrow next to Search, and then click Advanced Search.**

What is Advanced Search?
Advanced search will only search within your friends and people from Rio Grande Valley, TX.

Search within  My Networks & Friends  ▾

| Basic Info: | Name | | Interested In | |
| | Sex | | Relationship Status | |
| | Female ▾ | | Married ▾ | |
| | Home Town | | Looking For | |
| | Brownsville | | | |
| | Home State | | Political Views | |
| | ▾ | | | |
| | Home Country | | Religious Views | |
| | ▾ | | ▾ | |
| Contact Info: | Email | | City | |
| | Screen Name | | State | |
| | | | ▾ | |
| | Mobile | | Country | |
| | | | ▾ | |

2. **On the page that appears, use the drop-down lists and text fields to tell Facebook what kind of people you're looking for; then scroll down to the bottom of the page and click Advanced Search.** Facebook returns a clickable list of all the people in your network (and on your Friend List) that match the criteria you typed in, ordered by the number of criteria matched. (You see the criteria that matched high-lighted in yellow.)

Searching for people from your networks who match the following:                    Edit Advanced Search

| Sex: Female | Home Town: Brownsville | Relationship Status: Married |

Found 41 profile matches including 1 friend.                                         **1** 2 3 Next

| | | |
|---|---|---|
| Name: | **Patsy Alvarado** | Send Message |
| Network: | Rio Grande Valley, TX | Poke Her! |
| Matches: | Sex, Home Town, Home Town and Relationship Status | View Friends |
| | | Remove Friend |

| | | |
|---|---|---|
| Name: | **Adanela Alaniz** | Send Message |
| Network: | Rio Grande Valley, TX | Poke Her! |
| Matches: | Sex, Home Town, Home Town and Relationship Status | View Friends |
| | | Add to Friends |

| | | |
|---|---|---|
| Name: | **Ivonne Baiq** | Send Message |
| Networks: | Rio Grande Valley, TX | Poke Her! |
| | Texas Staff | View Friends |
| Matches: | Sex, Home Town, Home Town and Relationship Status | Add to Friends |

| | | |
|---|---|---|
| Name: | **Chrissy Boteler** | Send Message |
| Network: | Rio Grande Valley, TX | |

**Note** Dating? Facebook's browse feature (click the down arrow next to Search, and then click Browse) displays all the people in your primary network and then lets you either scroll through all the profile pictures, or search for potential sweeties based on a handful of criteria like age, sex, and the kind of relationship people are looking for.

# Inviting People to Be Your Friend

You can't just add people to your Friend List willy-nilly; they have to be Facebook members already, *and* they have to agree to be added.

**Note** Page 41 shows you how to invite non-Facebook members to join the site.

To invite a Facebook member to be your friend:

1. **Search for the person you want to befriend (see page 42).**

**Note** If you send a friend request to someone who can't normally see your profile—
they're not in your network, for example—Facebook temporarily grants that
person access to your profile so she can make an informed decision about whether
or not to accept your invitation. If you don't want folks to have this temporary
access, you can remove or customize it: On the Facebook main menu, click
"privacy", and then click "Poke, Message and Friend Request" (see Chapter 13).

2. **If your search returns the person you're looking for, click the "Add
   [member] as a Friend link" you see just below the profile picture.**
   If you don't find the person you're looking for, you can send her an
   invitation to join Facebook (page 41).

3. **Fill out the confirmation box that appears and then click Add
   Friend.** When you do, Facebook automatically sends an invitation to
   your would-be friend's email address *and* posts a friend request to her
   Facebook profile (page 6). If your friend agrees to the friendship and
   responds either to the email or the Facebook request (page 45), Facebook adds your name to her list of friends, and her name to yours. Facebook also sends you a *notification* (see page 81).

**Note** If you don't see the Add Friend link, it's because the person you're trying to
befriend has adjusted her privacy settings to block friend requests. See Chapter 13
for details.

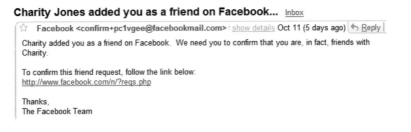

## Add Carmen as a friend?

You are about to add Carmen as a friend. We will then notify Carmen, who will have to confirm that you are friends.

[ add a personal message ]

**Security Check**

Enter **both** words below, separated by a **space.** What's This?
Can't read this? Try another.

toally    men's

Sick of these? Verify your account.

Text in the box:

Add Friend    Cancel

---

**Note** In its quest to support polite social interactions, Facebook doesn't give members a way to explicitly reject friend invitations, but they *can* ignore invitations. If you've sent an invitation and haven't heard back after a few days, try sending the person a message or a poke (page 66). Still no answer? Sorry—you've been snubbed.

# Responding to Friend Requests

When someone tries to add you to her Friend List, two things happen: Facebook sends you an email invitation, and it posts a little notice on your profile telling you that you have a friend request.

At that point, you've got two choices: You can confirm the request or ignore it, either in Facebook or right from your email program.

## Confirming Email Requests

If you're the type of person who checks her email every hour (or every five minutes) but only logs onto Facebook every couple of days, you'll want to handle friend requests from inside your email program. Here's how:

1. **Look in your email program for a message with the subject "[Somebody] added you as a friend on Facebook".**

   **Charity Jones added you as a friend on Facebook...** Inbox

   ☆ Facebook <confirm+pc1vgee@facebookmail.com> ⁙ show details Oct 11 (5 days ago) ↰ Reply |

   Charity added you as a friend on Facebook. We need you to confirm that you are, in fact, friends with Charity.

   To confirm this friend request, follow the link below:
   http://www.facebook.com/n/?reqs.php

   Thanks,
   The Facebook Team

2. **Open the email message and click the confirmation link.** Doing so whisks you to the Facebook page where you can confirm your friendship (see the next section).

## Confirming Requests in Facebook

Some people log in to Facebook whenever they're in front of a computer. If you're one of them, it's easier to respond to friend requests from your Facebook home page than to fire up your email program and wade through your inbox looking for invitations. To confirm a friend request from inside Facebook:

1. **Surf to your Facebook home page (click the "home" link in the upper-right part of your screen) and click the "friend request" link.** Friend requests appear on the upper-right side of your home page under Requests. (If you don't have any friend requests, you won't see any listed under Requests.)

2. **Make sure you want to accept the request, and then click Confirm.** If you've never heard of the person, the message he sent doesn't make sense, and the two of you have no friends in common, then you probably want to click the person's name and check out his profile to make sure the request is on the up-and-up.

Turn on the "[Name] can only see my limited profile" checkbox to pare down the personal details your new friend will be able to see (Chapter 13). You might want to do this if you've got a few social circles going on Facebook and don't want them to collide. For example, if the friend request is from your boss, then you don't want her browsing through your political rants or stag-party photos.

3. **In the confirmation box that appears, turn on the checkbox next to the description that best fits your relationship—if you want.** Depending on which box you check, Facebook may display extra (optional) fields you can use to describe your relationship in more detail. Check Worked Together, for example, and Facebook displays fields you can use to indicate that you've worked together for five years and are still working for Acme Foods.

If you don't want the world to know how you know this person (you "hooked up" with him but have too much class to advertise that fact, say), click Skip This Step instead of following steps 3–4. You still become friends with him, but Facebook doesn't list how you know him.

**How do you know Emily Moore?**

☐ Lived together      ☐ In my family
☐ Worked together      ☐ Through a friend
☐ From an organization or team      ☐ Through Facebook
☐ Took a course together      ☐ Met randomly
☐ From a summer / study abroad program      ☐ We hooked up
☐ Went to school together      ☐ We dated
☐ Traveled together      ☐ I don't even know this person.

[ Request Confirmation ] [ Skip This Step ]

The details you supply in this box are what make up your (and your friend's) *social timelines* (page 54).

4. **Click Skip This Step.** Just like that, you're Facebook friends.

If you want your friend to confirm the details of your relationship, click Request Confirmation instead of Skip This Step. (Confirmed relationship details appear on both Friend Lists in black, unconfirmed in gray.)

**You are now friends with** Emil

f **View her profile**

📟 **Write on her wall**

✉ **Send her a message**

---

**Tip** To see what friends you and your new friend have in common, simply click "View her profile," and then, on your new friend's profile, hunt for the Mutual Friends section (it's below her profile picture).

## Ignoring a Friend Request

In Facebook as in life, there will be times when someone extends the hand of friendship and you just don't want to shake it. After all, confirming a friend request doesn't just give your new pal access to a big chunk of your personal life; it also lets the world know that you think enough of the guy to declare yourself his friend. If you receive a friend request from someone you've never heard of, say, or whose profile paints a picture so creepy you want to lock your virtual door, all you have to do is quietly remove all traces of the request and get on with your life.

To do so:

1. **Sign in to Facebook (page 221) if you're not already there.** *Don't* follow the link inside the friend request email you received, or you'll confirm the friendship.

2. **In the notifications section of your Facebook home page, click the "friend request" link.**

3. **In the box that appears, click Ignore.** That's all you have to do: Facebook immediately removes the friend request link from your home page.

---

**Note** The guy who sent the invitation won't be notified that you've officially ignored him; he just won't receive a confirmation.

---

4. **In your email program, delete the friend request email.**

# Viewing Your Friends

Facebook automatically displays six randomly selected friends from your primary network (Chapter 2) in the Friends section of your profile.

To see more than these six friends listed on your profile—or to see more details about each of your friends—you've got a few options. You can:

- **See all of your friends at one fell swoop.** To do so, head to the Friends section of your profile and click the See All link. When you do, Facebook displays your All Friends list. (If you know you have more friends than Facebook displays, make sure the Everyone tab is selected.) Another way to see your All Friends list is to head to the top of any Facebook screen, click the down arrow next to Friends, and then click All Friends.

- **See friends who've changed their profiles lately.** From your All Friends list, click the Recently Updated tab. (Alternatively, head to the top of any Facebook page and click Friends.)

- **See friends who've updated their statuses recently.** From your All Friends list, click the Status Updates tab to see your friends' late-breaking statuses.

- **See friends who are online right this minute.** From your All Friends list, click the "More…" tab. Then, from the Show drop-down list, choose Online Now.

- **See your friends broken out by the network they belong to, or whether they're college friends, work friends, or friends who live close to you.** From your All Friends list, click the "More…" tab. Then, from the Show drop-down list, choose a specific network (to see friends who belong to that network), College Friends (to see friends who belong to college networks), Work Friends (to see friends who belong to work-related networks), of Regional Friends (to see friends who belong to geographical networks).

> **Note** When you choose College Friends, Work Friends, or Regional Friends, Facebook displays an additional field you can use to show only those pals who belong to a specific college, work, or regional network.

# Organizing Your Friends

The options Facebook gives you for viewing your friends (page 49) are great if you have only a handful of pals. But if you're a hardcore social butterfly with dozens or even hundreds of friends, you'll want to organize your friends into separate lists that reflect how you categorize them in your mind.

For example, imagine that in addition to your workplace network, you're involved in a book club, a softball league, and a 12-step program. Creating four separate lists lets you keep track of your different social circles at a glance. And because Facebook lets you send the same message to all the friends on a single list all at once (see page 60) and even invite everyone on the list to join the same group (page 103) or event (119), creating separate Friend Lists helps you communicate with folks quicker while reducing the risk of having your worlds collide.

## Creating a New Friend List

Facebook lets you create up to 100 different Friend Lists, each of which can contain up to 1,500 names. (Of course, unless you're a politician, you probably won't need anywhere near that many.) Here's how to create a new Friend List:

1. **Head to the top of any Facebook page and click Friends.** Head to the right side of the page that appears and click "Make a New List" (page 49).

> **Note** Because lists were designed to help you manage a bunch of friends, you don't see the "Make a New List" link unless you have 11 or more Facebook friends.

2. **In the field that appears, type in a name for your list and hit Return.** In the example on the next page, the list's name is moms.

3. **Add the names of some friends to your list.** The easiest way is to click the Select Multiple Friends link and then, from the list of thumbnails that appears, click the friends you want to add to your list. (Clicking a thumbnail once turns it blue to let you know you've selected it; clicking again de-selects it.) When you finish, click Save List. Your newly created list appears on the All Friends page beneath the Friend Lists heading.

**Note** Alternatively, you can click in the Add to List field and type in names one at a time.

**Note** You can add the same friend to multiple Friend Lists.

## Viewing a Friend List

Friend Lists are for your eyes only—your friends never see which lists, if any, you've added them to. To see all the friends on a particular Friend List:

1. **Go to the top of any Facebook page and click Friends.**

2. **Head to the right side of the page that appears and click the name of the list you want to see.** Facebook displays the names of the friends you've added to that list.

## Editing a Friend List

Online or off, social circles and friendships change over time. After you've created a Friend List (page 51), you can change its name, add friends to it, or delete friends from it.

To change the name of a list:

1. **Go to the top of any Facebook page and click Friends.**

2. **Head to the right side of the page that appears and click the "edit" link next to the name of the list you want to change.**

3. **In the field that appears, type the new name. When you finish, hit Enter.**

You add friends to an existing list the same way you add them to a new list (see page 52).

To delete friends from a list:

1. **First, view the list (page 52).**

2. **Scroll down to the friend you want to remove from the list and click the X Facebook displays to the right of the friend's name.** Then, in the confirmation box that appears, click "Remove from List".

## Deleting a Friend List

Maybe you created a Friend List and find you never use it. Or maybe the number of friends on one of your Friend Lists dwindled to nothing. For whatever reason, deleting a Friend List is easy:

1. **View the list you want to delete (page 52).**

2. **Scroll down to the bottom of the list and click the "Delete this list" link.** Then, in the confirmation box that appears, click Delete List.

# Viewing Your Connections to Friends

If you have a lot of Facebook friends (or a bad memory), you might be interested in viewing your *social timeline*. A social timeline is simply a list of your Facebook friends arranged chronologically by when you met—based on the relationship details you've given Facebook (page 47)—accompanied by how-we-met details. Viewing your social timeline is easy and kind of fun. At the top of any Facebook screen, click the down arrow next to Friends, and then choose All Friends. Then click the "More..." tab and, from the Show drop-down list, select Social Timeline.

From Facebook's point of view, understanding how people connect is incredibly useful (all the better to sell you stuff, my dear—see page 177). From your point of view, looking at your social timeline is like looking through shoeboxes of old pictures. You're not going to want to do it every day, but every once in a blue moon you may find it interesting to browse through your timeline and settle a bet over which of two friends you met first, or realize that you tend to connect with people based only on one or two shared interests.

> **Note** Looking at your social timeline will be about as interesting as watching paint dry unless you have a lot of Facebook friends *and* you (or your friends) have been diligent about providing Facebook with relationship details (page 47).

## Adding Relationship Details

Because your social timeline is basically a list of relationship details, you have to cough up some details before you can see your timeline. If you or your friends didn't enter relationship details during the befriending process (page 47), no sweat—you can add them any time. Here's how:

1. **At the top of any Facebook screen, click the down arrow next to Friends, and then click All Friends to display your Friend List.**

2. **For each friend in your Friend List, click the square "expand" icon on the right side of the listing, and then click the Details link, which either reads "[ edit details ]" or "How do you know [Name]?"**

3. **In the box that appears, turn on as many checkboxes as you like, and then click Request Confirmation.** Facebook shoots your friend a quick email (as well as a Facebook notification) she can use to confirm what you've written.

**How do you know Patsy Alvarado?**

☐ Lived together  
☐ Worked together  
☑ From an organization or team  

    Which organization or team? optional  
    RGV mom's play group  
    When was this? optional  
    2007 ▾ to Present ▾  
    + Add another organization or team  

☐ Took a course together  
☐ From a summer / study abroad program  
☐ Went to school together  
☐ Traveled together  

☑ In my family  
    How are you related? optional  
    [_____ ▾]  

☐ Through a friend  
☐ Through Facebook  
☑ Met randomly  
    What's the story here? optional  
    [_____]  
    What year was this? optional  
    [_____ ▾]  

☐ We hooked up  
☐ We dated  
☐ I don't even know this person.  

[ Request Confirmation ] [ Cancel ]

**Note** The details you add show up on your Friend List and profile as well as on your friend's Friend List and profile, even if your friend doesn't confirm them. The difference? Details appear in gray until they're confirmed; after that, they appear in black.

# Breaking Up: Unfriending Friends

Breaking up is never easy, but sometimes it has to be done. Say one of your Facebook friends stabs you in the electronic back by posting inappropriate stuff on your wall (page 67) or spamming all your other friends, and you really have no choice but to cut him loose. To remove someone from your Friend List:

1. **From your Friend List (page 52), click the name or photo of the person you want to "unfriend."** Facebook pops up the person's profile.

2. **Scroll down to the bottom of the profile and click the "Remove from Friends" link.** (You don't see this link on profiles of non-friends.) You're friends no more.

> **Note** Unlike quietly ignoring a friend request, removing someone from your Friend List sends a clear message. Because Facebook friendship is reciprocal, removing a friend means you disappear from your former friend's Friend List—an unmistakable rebuff.

**4**

# Sending Messages to Friends

Just like your regular email program, Facebook lets you send private messages to other Facebook members. Great, you're probably thinking, just what I need: yet another inbox to check. But before you skip ahead to the next chapter, you might want to give these tools a chance. First off, Facebook makes exchanging messages dead simple—even easier than regular email. And then there are the slightly zany—but slightly addictive—ways to keep in touch with others that no email program can match. In an effort to mimic the different ways we interact with each other in real life, Facebook lets you *poke* (give a virtual "hey, how ya doin'?'" wave to) friends; write on their virtual message boards; and even send whimsical digital gifts. Even if you're not persuaded by any of this, it's still worth understanding the messaging system since, soon enough, you'll no doubt get a Facebook message from one of your own friends.

# Sending Messages

Lots of Web sites offer free Web-based email, and Facebook is one of them—sort of. As a Facebook member, you can send private messages to any other Facebook member (whether or not they're on your Friend List), and to regular email addresses. But only other Facebook members can send *you* Facebook messages. In other words, when you register for Facebook, you don't get a *YourName@Facebook.com* email account; people have to sign up for Facebook and follow the steps below if they want to send a message to your Facebook inbox.

> **Note** Facebook temporarily grants your message recipients limited access to your profile, even if they normally can't see it (because, for example, you've *blocked* them [see page 236]). To prevent or customize this temporary access, mouse up to the top-right part of any Facebook screen, click "privacy", and then click "Poke, Message and Friend Request" (see page 230 for the details).

## Sending Messages to Friends

Most of the messages you send, of course, will be to people you already know. Facebook gives you a simple set of tools that will look familiar to anyone who's used email before. Here's what you do:

1. **At the top of any Facebook screen, click the down arrow next to Inbox, and then click Compose Message on the drop-down menu.** Or, you can click the word Inbox and then click the Compose Message tab on the right side of the page that appears.

2. **On the Compose Message page, start typing your friend's name (if she's a Facebook member), email address (for non-Facebook members), or the name of a Friend List (page 52).** As soon as you begin typing, Facebook displays a list of your friends and Friend Lists. To select a name, click it or use the up and down arrow keys to select the name, and then hit Enter. If you're sending a message to a non-Facebook member, simply type in the person's full email address. You

can add multiple recipients, if you like; just hit the Tab key after each recipient, and Facebook takes care of the rest. (See page 63 for more on sending messages to multiple people.)

Why would you want to use Facebook to send a message to someone who's not a Facebook member? Two reasons: First, you're already in Facebook and don't want to waste time switching over to your email program (or can't, if you're using someone else's computer). Second, you want to lure this non-member friend into your Facebook social circle by giving her a taste of Facebook's coolness. When your friend clicks the Facebook-generated "Click to Reply" link in your email, she's whisked to a Facebook page she can use to preview Facebook messaging, as well as to get more info and sign up.

**Tip** After you've added a recipient's name, you can delete it by clicking the "X" Facebook displays after each name, or hitting the Delete key.

| Inbox | Sent Messages | Notifications | | Compose Message |

To: |
Start typing a friend's name or email address
Subject:
Message:

Attach: ⌷ Share Link

Send    Cancel

3. **Fill in the Subject line and type your message.** Then, if you want to pass along a link to a Web site (or to a photo or video on the Web), click Share Link (page 69). When you finish, click Send.

4. **If a security box like the one on page 67 appears, type in the security words you see and click Submit.** Facebook sends your message and stores a copy in your Sent Messages tab, which you can view by heading to the top of any Facebook screen and clicking the down arrow next to Inbox, and then clicking Sent Messages.

## Sending Messages to People You're Not (Yet) Friends With

Facebook lets you send a message to *any* Facebook member, even if she's not on your Friend List and doesn't belong to any of your networks.

To send a message to a non-friend Facebook member:

1. **Surf either to the profile of the person you want to contact (page 36), or the person's listing on your search or browse page (page 42).**

2. **Click either the "Send [Name] a Message" link (which you find on a person's profile) or the Send Message link (which you find in search results).** Whichever link you click, up pops the Compose Message tab. Type your message and send it off as explained on page 61.

To: Robert Redfordman

Subject:

Message:

Send    Cancel

## Sending a Message to More Than One Person

Because Facebook was designed to help people communicate online just as they do offline, the site makes it easy to send a message to an individual—but a little harder to send the same message to dozens of people all at once. If you go too far down that path, the Facebook design team reasoned, you're talking spam. After all, how often do you whip out a bullhorn and address a real-life crowd of dozens?

To send messages to your friends all at once, you first need to create a Friend List (page 51). Then, on the Compose Message tab, head to the To field and type the name of the list.

**Note** Another exception to the no-spam rule is that Facebook lets you send the same message to every member of a *group* (page 103)—although even then, Facebook theoretically caps the number of group recipients at 1,000. (The cap is theoretical because some Facebook members have had their accounts suspended for sending messages to a lot fewer than 1,000 people.)

# Receiving Messages

When someone sends you a message via Facebook, two things happen:

- **You receive the message in your Facebook inbox.** To open your inbox, head to the main menu and click Inbox. Then click either the subject line or the first line of any message to see it in its entirety, as shown on page 65.

- **You receive the message in your regular email program.** Facebook sends the message to your primary email address.

**Joice Templeton sent you a message on Facebook...** Inbox | X

☆ Facebook to me        show details 10:31 PM (2 minutes ago) ↩ Reply | ▼

Joice sent you a message.

Subject: Farmer's Market meeting

"I was hoping to get together with you before the meeting next Friday to go over a contact list of area farmers. Call me..."

To reply to this message, follow the link below:
http://www.facebook.com/n/?inbox/readmessage.php&t=6401843087

___

Want to control which emails you receive from Facebook? Go to: http://www.facebook.com /editaccount.php?notifications

**Email Notifications**

Facebook notifies you by email whenever actions are taken on Facebook that involve you. You can control which email notifications you receive.

Email me at **eamoore68@gmail.com** when someone...

☑ Sends me a message
☑ Adds me as a friend
☑ Writes on my Wall

# Viewing Your Facebook Inbox

It's easy to tell if you have a new Facebook message even without opening your inbox. Just take a look the blue main menu bar at the top of any Facebook screen. If you see a number in parentheses right after the word Inbox, you've got a new message (or two, or more). Click Inbox, and a list of messages appears.

| Profile edit | Friends ▼ | Networks ▼ | Inbox (2) ▼ | | home | account | privacy | logout |

| Inbox | Sent Messages | Notifications | | | Compose Message |

Select: --- ▼  Mark as Unread  Mark as Read  Delete

| ● ☐ | Patsy Alvarado<br>Today at 5:11 pm | re: Park hang?<br>I was wondering what you thought of taking some food to t... | x |
| ● ☐ | Melissa, Charity, Dabne...<br>Today at 5:05 pm | RE: Meetup website<br>THat's a great idea, but I think we should delete this th... | x |
| ☐ | Dabney Holtzman<br>Today at 9:07 am | re: Hope your little one feels better...<br>I'm jealous. I could use alittle fresh air and sunshine. ... | x |

Facebook puts a big blue dot in front of any message you haven't read yet, and highlights the entire listing in light blue. You can choose to see a list of only the messages you've already read, only the ones you *haven't* read, or all your messages (you see all of them unless you choose a different option from the Select drop-down list). Clicking a sender's name or picture shoots you directly to that person's profile, which is handy if you don't recognize him.

> **Note** A little left arrow in front of a message listing means you've replied to the message. Clicking the X on the right side of a listing deletes the *thread* that message belongs to. (A *thread* is a bunch of messages with the same subject line.)

## Reading and Responding to Messages

To read a message in your inbox, click either the subject line or first line of the message and Facebook displays the whole message.

> **Note** A particularly cool feature of Facebook's inbox is that when you display a message that's the latest in a long, drawn-out, back-and-forth thread, Facebook zips you down to the latest message—you don't have to read through the long list of exchanges and hunt for the latest one yourself.

To reply to the message, simply type your response in the Reply box, and then click Send. To delete the message without replying, click Delete.

Attach:   Share Link

Send    Back to Inbox     Mark as Unread   Delete

# Poking

*Poking* sounds a lot more provocative than it is. Giving someone a *poke* in Facebook is nothing more than the electronic equivalent of asking someone, "Hey, what's up?" Pokes appear as a "You were poked by [name]" message on the recipient's home page.

> **Tip**   Poking—like sneaking up behind someone and tapping her shoulder—isn't really good for much beyond the yuk factor. Depending on you and your pals' tolerance for friendly nudging, poking either gets the award for Silliest Social Aid or Most Annoying Thing Ever. If you're in the latter camp, you'll find *notifications* (page 81) similar but more useful.

**Pokes**

You were poked by
Emily Moore.
poke back | remove poke

> **Note**   You can poke any Facebook member you like; you don't have to be friends with the pokee or belong to the same network. But if you poke someone who doesn't normally have access to your profile, be aware that he'll be able to see your profile for a week post-poke—unless you explicitly tell Facebook otherwise (see page 230). But letting a pokee see your profile is rarely a problem. After all, if you're that worried somebody might discover your passion for the Bay City Rollers, you shouldn't poke him in the first place.

To poke someone:

1. **Find the person you want to poke by viewing your Friend List (page 52) or using Facebook's Search box (page 36).**

2. **Click the "Poke Her!" (or "Poke Him!") link on the intended recipient's profile (page 6) or on your Friend List (page 52).** (On your Friend List, you have to expand the person's listing [see page 55], and the link simply reads "Poke".)

Send Patsy a Gift
Send Patsy a Message
( Poke Her! )

3. **If a security box appears, type in the Security Check words, and then click Poke.** You briefly see a "You have poked [name]" message, and the damage is done: Your poke message appears on the pokee's home page, complete with a link she can use to poke you back.

**Poke Joice?**

? You are about to poke Joice. They will be informed of this the next time they log in.

Also, if you poke Joice, they will be able to see your profile for one week. Edit Privacy

**Security Check**
Enter **both** words below, separated by a **space.** What's This?
Can't read this? Try another.

Sized    Javits

Sick of these? Verify your account.

Text in the box:

Poke    Cancel

# Writing on Walls

One of the sections on every Facebook member's profile is a forum called the *wall*. A wall is a place for your Facebook pals to share interesting photos, videos, Web sites, and character insights. By default, the only peoples' walls you can write on are your own and your friends'. But since walls are part of profiles, anyone who can view your profile can see your wall messages. You can think of walls as a 21st-century version of the dry-erase message boards they used to have in dorm rooms: an informal place to brag, tease, show solidarity, get attention, and occasionally impart useful information.

**Note** If you check out the *Applications Directory* (page 207), you can find several Facebook applications (such as FunWall, SuperWall, and Graffiti) that let you add photos, video clips, and even "spray paint" on your friends' walls.

**Note** Because friendly jokes can sometimes get out of hand, Facebook lets you remove any wall posts you don't like (page 70) and restrict who can see your wall (page 224).

## Writing on a Friend's Wall

Writing on a friend's wall is a more public way of expressing yourself than sending your friend a message, because all your friend's friends will see your wall post. Good candidates for wall posts include thanks, congratulations, birthday greetings, and other tidbits your shared connections might find interesting or useful.

**Note** To write on your own wall, follow the steps below, but head to your own profile instead of a friend's.

To write on a friend's wall:

1. **On your friend's profile, scroll down to the Wall section, where you should see a text box that says "Write something..."** If you don't see the text box, you're out of luck: Your friend has restricted access to her wall.

2. **Type your message in the text box.**

3. **If you want to add a link to an online photo, video, or Web site, click Share Link, fill out the box that appears, and then click Attach.** You can't use this method to share photos or videos that are saved on your computer—they have to be posted online somewhere. If you want to upload photos stored on your computer, flip to page 163.

**Tip** You can skip the http:// part of the Web site address if you like—Facebook automatically adds it for you.

> **Share Link**
>
> Share a Photo, Video, or Link:
>
> http://www.sandcastledays.com/
>
> Attach    Cancel

4. **If you decided to share a link, choose which thumbnail you want to accompany your link.** Facebook pulls a site description and a handful of thumbnails from the site for you to choose from. To skip the graphic, turn on the No Picture checkbox.

**Tip** If you change your mind about sharing a link, click the "remove" link.

> **▼ The Wall**
>
> Displaying all 5 wall posts.                                    See All
>
> Sand castle days at the Sheraton--wonder how mobbed it will be?
>
> remove
>
> Choose a Thumbnail    **South Padre Island Texas Sand Castle Days Fall Family Festival' October 18-21, 2007**
>
> ◄ ► 1 of 4    Sand sculpture competition and fall family festival with music, beach games, venders, and amazing sand creations from international artists.
> http://www.sandcastledays.com/
>
> ☐ No Picture
>
> Post

5. **Click Post.** Your message appears on your friend's wall.

**Emily Moore** shared a link
at 11:00pm

Sand castle days at the Sheraton--wonder
how mobbed it will be?

South Padre Island Texas Sand Castle D...

Write on My Wall - Delete

> **Note** Some Facebook applications (page 206) let you attach additional stuff to the messages you post on people's walls. The Graffiti Wall application, for example, lets you decorate your friend's wall with virtual spray paint.

## Responding to a Wall Post

When someone writes on your wall, you can have a chuckle and leave it at that—or you can respond in one of the following ways:

**Patsy Alvarado wrote**
at 10:01pm on October 15th, 2007

Don't the kids look cute! I'll give you a copy when I get a chance
to develop them.

Wall-to-Wall - Write on Patsy's Wall - Message - Delete

- **Write something on the poster's wall.** Clicking "Wall-to-Wall" displays a history of your and your friend's posts to each other's walls, and lets you add a new post. Clicking "Write on [your friend's] Wall" skips the back-and-forth history and just lets you type in your post.

- **Send the poster a private Facebook message.** Click Message; page 60 covers Facebook messaging.

- **Delete the post.** You can delete any post from your own wall, no matter who posted it. To do so, simply click Delete, and then click Delete again in the confirmation box.

> **Note** You can also delete messages you posted on a friend's wall. To do so, surf to that person's profile, scroll down to the wall post you want to delete, and then click Delete.

# Sending Gifts

A Facebook *gift* is a greeting card–style icon you can send to someone, accompanied by a personal message. You can choose from hundreds of professionally-designed graphics, most of them of the smiley-face-and-teddy-bear variety. After you send a gift, it appears on the recipient's profile—in the Gifts section, on the recipient's wall, or both, depending on whether you decide to make the gift *public* or *private*.

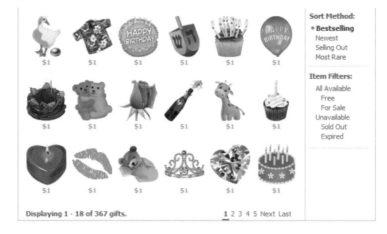

> **Note** Like pokes, gifts are endearing niceties with little purpose beyond making people smile.

Facebook lets you send one gift for free; after that, you have to pony up— typically, one dollar per gift.

> **Note** To get around the $1 price tag, click the Free link to see the occasional freebies that appear. You can also check out the Free Gifts application (see page 206).

To send someone a Facebook gift:

1. **On your profile, scroll down until you see the Gifts section (you may have to click the blue Gifts header to see the entire Gifts section), and then click "Give a Gift".**

**Note** Gifts is a built-in Facebook application (page 206), which means you (or someone with access to your Facebook account) can delete it from your account. If you don't see the Gifts section on your profile, head to www.facebook.com/giftshop.php.

2. **In the page that appears, find the gift you want to give, and then click it.** If you don't see anything you want to give, click one of the links in the bottom-right part of the page to see more gifts.

3. **Once you've selected your gift, use the "Choose your recipient" drop-down list to tell Facebook who to send the gift to. Then type in the message you want to accompany it.**

4. **Decide whether to hide your gift from prying eyes.** Nobody's going to be embarrassed by an "Attaboy, Ralph!" or a "Happy Graduation, Linda!," but some of the more...specialized icons may reflect poorly on the receiver—especially if she uses Facebook to get gigs or conduct business. When in doubt, choose Private. When you send a gift privately, everybody who can see the recipient's profile can see the gift, but only the recipient can see the accompanying message and who sent it.

> **Note** If you receive an embarrassing gift, you can hide your entire Gift section. To do so: On your profile, click the X on the right side of the blue Gifts heading. Then, in the confirmation box that appears, click Remove Box.

5. **Click Continue.**

6. **Fill out your credit card information, and then click Purchase and Send Gift.** You may not be asked for this information the first time around, since Facebook lets most members send one gift for free.

**Payment:**

| | |
|---|---|
| Cardholder's Name: | Emily Moore |
| Credit Card Type: | Visa ▾ |
| Credit Card Number: | |
| Expiration Date: | 01 ▾  2007 ▾ |
| Country: | United States ▾ |
| Address: | |
| City/Town: | |
| State/Province/Region: | |
| Zip/Postal Code: | |

☑ Save this information for future Facebook purchases

☐ Use a coupon code

**Buy in Advance and Save:**

☐ Add 10 gift credits to my account for $5.00 USD (what's a gift credit?)

**Total: $1.00** USD

[ Purchase and Send Gift ]   [ < Edit Gift ]

By purchasing a gift, you are agreeing to the Facebook Terms of Sale.
Having problems? Click here for help.

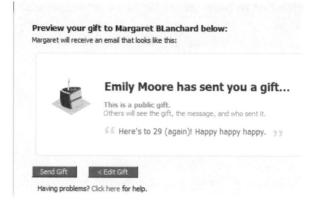

**Preview your gift to Margaret BLanchard below:**

Margaret will receive an email that looks like this:

**Emily Moore has sent you a gift...**

This is a public gift.
Others will see the gift, the message, and who sent it.

❝ Here's to 29 (again)! Happy happy happy. ❞

Send Gift    < Edit Gift

Having problems? Click here for help.

7. **In the confirmation box that appears, double-check your handi-work and, if it looks good, click Send Gift.** (If you want to make changes, click Edit Gift instead.) Up pops a box letting you know the gift has been sent, complete with a link you can click to view the gift on the recipient's profile.

Emily Moore wrote
at 11:33pm

Here's to 29 (again!) Happy happy happy

Wall-to-Wall · Write on My Wall · Delete

# Exchanging Automatic Updates

**R**emember what keeping up with your friends *used to* require? Time-consuming emails (*Sorry it's been so long...*), potentially intrusive instant messages (*hello? u there?*), even the occasional in-person visit. No more. Thanks to Facebook's easy-to-activate broadcast and subscription tools, staying in touch is easier than ever. *Subscriptions* and *notifications,* for example, alert you when, say, your best friend uploads a new picture, your softball coach gets off work, or your study buddy posts his analysis of Macbeth. This chapter shows you how to sign up for and tweak these handy updates.

# Types of Updates

Facebook offers four different ways you can get details about your friends' activities. Three (*news feeds*, *mini-feeds*, and *notifications*) appear automatically—on your home page, your profile, and your notification inbox, respectively.

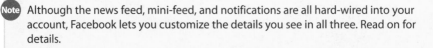

**Note** Although the news feed, mini-feed, and notifications are all hard-wired into your account, Facebook lets you customize the details you see in all three. Read on for details.

If you prefer to keep up with your pals without having to log in to Facebook, you can choose to sign up for customized Web feeds called *subscriptions*.

**Note** Facebook offers one other kind of automatic update: It tells you when friends' birthdays are coming up. If you check the Birthdays section of your home page (it's on the right-hand side) every time you sign on, you'll never again forget a friend's birthday.

# News Feeds: What Others Are Doing

*News feeds* are constantly updated lists of the things your Facebook friends are doing on the site: adding applications, writing on walls, commenting on notes and photos, and so on. Your news feed appears automatically on your Facebook home page, front and center—you don't need to do anything special to see it. Facebook doesn't let you do away with your news feed, but you can customize it to show more (or less) of the activities—and the friends—you're interested in.

# Customizing Your News Feed

In every social circle, you're bound to have some friends you're closer to than others. If you'd prefer to concentrate on just two or three friends' activities—or skip the who's-dating-who-this-week chatter and focus just on the groups or events your friends are involved with—you can do so by customizing your news feed. Here's how:

1. **From your home page, head to the News Feed section and click the Preferences link.**

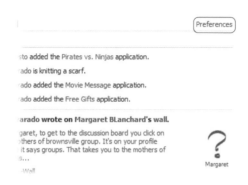

2. **On the page that appears, tell Facebook what you want to see more of on your news feed, and what you want to see less of.** Drag the sliders up to see more event-related news, group-related news, and so on, and drag them down to see less.

> **Tip** Mouse over each Story Types icon to see a quickie highlighted description of each news category you can customize using its slider.

To see more news about certain friends, head to the More About These Friends section in the lower-left part of the page; type in a friend's name, and then click Add. To see less about certain friends, do the same in the lower-right Less About These Friends section. After you make each change, Facebook pops up a temporary Saved Setting message (or Restored Setting message, if you clicked Undo Last).

**Story Types**

Drag these sliders up or down to indicate which types of stories you'd like to see more or less often in comparison to one another. These preferences will take effect the next time you get new stories. To control which stories your friends see, use the Feed Privacy page.

| Story Types | 31 | 👥 | 🖼 | ☐ | ♥ | 👥 | 💬 | ✏ | 👤 | 🔲 |
|---|---|---|---|---|---|---|---|---|---|---|
| 🗐 Show More | | | | | | | | | | |
| Default | ═ | ═ | ═ | ═ | ═ | ═ | ═ | ═ | ═ | ═ |
| 🗐 Show Less | | | | | | | | | | |

How do I use this?                                                    Undo Last | Reset All

**🗐 More About These Friends**

You can select up to 20 friends that you find interesting. You will get News Feed stories about these people more frequently.

**Person:** Start typing a friend's name  [Add]

More About...

　　　Patsy Alvarado remove
　　　Margaret BLanchard remove

**🗐 Less About These Friends**

You can select up to 20 friends that you prefer not to see in your News Feed. You will only get stories about these people if nothing else is available.

**Person:** Start typing a friend's name  [Add]

Less About...

　　　You have not added any friends

> **Note** News feeds work both ways: Facebook keeps track of *your* actions on the site, too, and includes them in your friends' news feeds. To learn how to prevent certain things you do from showing up on your friends' news feeds, see page 101.

# Mini-feeds: What You're Doing

Your news feed keeps track of all the stuff your friends do on Facebook. Similarly, your *mini-feed* (which appears on your profile page) chronicles the stuff *you* do on Facebook. Anyone who can see your profile can see your mini-feed.

> **Note** The mini-feed doesn't contain *additional* information; it just aggregates the juicy bits displayed elsewhere on your profile. So, what people can't see on your profile, they can't see on your mini-feed. For example, if you RSVP to a secret event and your friend Ralph wasn't invited, he won't be able to find out he was snubbed by reading your mini-feed.

## Customizing Your Mini-feed

You can customize the mini-feed that appears on your profile in two ways:

- **By removing individual stories.** Stories are specific actions you've taken on Facebook, such as updating your *status* (page 84) to "Heading home for the day."

- **By telling Facebook to leave out categories of actions.** You can tell Facebook to keep mum when you comment on a note or leave a group, for example.

To customize your mini-feed:

1. **On the Facebook main menu, click Profile.**

2. **Scroll down to the Mini-Feed section of your profile and read through the stories.** If you don't see any stories listed beneath the Mini-Feed heading, click the right-arrow to expand the section.

3. **Delete any stories you don't want people to see.** Click the X at the right end of a story snippet (and then, in the confirmation box that appears, click the Hide Story button) to delete that story from your mini-feed.

4. **Specify which types of actions you want to reveal in your mini-feed, and which you don't.** See page 101 for details.

# Facebook Notifications

A *notification* is a message telling you that something involving *you* happened on Facebook: Someone wrote on your wall, for example, or invited you to join a group, or replied to something you said on a discussion board.

# Viewing Your Notifications

Notifications appear in two places: in your regular email program's inbox, and on Facebook's Notifications tab. You also get a heads-up on your home page when you get a notification.

**Notifications**

📧 1 new notification

- **To see the email versions of your notifications,** head to your email program and view your emails just as you normally would.

- **To see your notifications in Facebook,** at the top of any Facebook screen, click the down arrow next to Inbox, and then choose Notifications from the drop-down menu. Make sure the Notifications tab is selected; if it's not, click it to select it. The little blue dot that appears in front of some notifications means that they're new. (The dot and the corresponding heads-up on your home page disappear after you display the Notifications tab.)

| Inbox | Sent Messages | **Notifications** | | Compose Message |
|---|---|---|---|---|

Today

● 📧 Lucy Krzywda has replied to your post on a discussion board 10:46am   x

Yesterday

📅 Margaret Blanchard wrote on the Wall for "Get Together at the "Zoo Boo"   x

Show notifications...

↳ ☑ Received
↵ ☑ Sent By Me

# Choosing Which Notifications You Want to See

Unless you tell it otherwise, Facebook assumes you want to be notified about a staggering amount of social minutia. This means that if you have more than two or three friends who actively use the site, your email inbox will overflow from all the notifications you'll receive.

To specify what you want to be notified about and what you don't, follow these steps:

1. **On the Facebook main menu, click "account".**

2. **On the page that appears, click the Notifications tab.**

3. **On the Email Notifications tab, turn on the Off radio box next to any activity you don't want to hear about, and then scroll down to the bottom of the page and click Save Changes.**

**Tip** Facebook always displays friend requests, invitations to groups and events, and photo tag requests (page 170) on your home page, so the notifications you get about these activities are redundant. Turn them off and you won't miss a thing (assuming you check your home page from time to time).

# Subscriptions

Technically, subscriptions are *Web feeds*—those ubiquitous summary blurbs provided by Web publishers like the *New York Times* and Reuters and known to geeks everywhere as RSS, which stands for Rich Site Summary or Really Simple Syndication depending on who you ask. Whatever you call them, think of a *subscription* as a continuously updated newsletter that's stored as a big chunk of data that you can format and view however you like— as a basic, no-frills list of items on a Web page, for example, or in a fancy online news reader.

> **Note** When you follow the steps on page 86, your subscription appears as a basic list on a Web page. To see it in a different format, check out one of the many free news reader (a.k.a. *aggregator*) programs and services, such as Bloglines (*www.bloglines.com*), Google Reader (*www.google.com/reader*), or Feed Demon (*www.newsgator.com*). For an in-depth look at all things Web feed, check out *http://oreilly.com/feeds*.

Subscriptions don't give you any info that you couldn't find by combing through Facebook, but they make that information easier to get to because it appears on a single Web page that updates automatically. Plus, you don't have to log in to Facebook to see it. And, depending on which Web browser you use, you can customize the way you see subscription info. For example, if you use Internet Explorer, you can sort subscription info, specify how often you want to see updates, and even play a sound when the info gets updated.

You can sign up for one or more of the following subscriptions:

- **A subscription that shows the current status of your friends.** A Facebook *status* is a quick one-liner that your friends type in from time to time, such as "I'm leaving work" or "I'm at the library." Signing up for a status subscription lets you track where your friends are and what they're doing at any given time without having to log in to Facebook.

**Note** To update your status: On your home page (get there by clicking the "home" link at the top of any Facebook screen), scroll to the Status Updates section and click the "What are you doing right now?" link. (If this isn't the first time you've updated your status, you'll see an "edit" link instead).

Type whatever you'd like in the box that appears (you can delete the word "is" if you want to use a different verb), or click the down arrow and choose something from the list (like "is at home" or "is at work"). When you're done, simply click somewhere else on your screen and Facebook updates your status so all your friends can see what you're up to. Click the "clear status" link to erase what you wrote in the box.

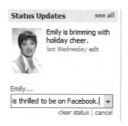

- **A subscription that shows you the stuff—Web links, photos, video links, and so on—your friends are posting, as they post it.** Because this kind of subscription gives you a one-stop shop for all the resources your friends are sharing, it's perfect for work and study groups.

**Note** To see how to post your own stuff, check out page 185.

- **A subscription that shows you the notes your friends (or other Facebook members) are publishing, as they publish them.** (Flip to page 90 to learn about Facebook notes.) Signing up for a notes subscription helps make sure you don't miss a single exciting install-ment of your friends' blogs (er, Facebook notes—see page 90), even when you're not logged in to Facebook. You can subscribe to notes published by any Facebook member who chooses to syndicate her notes (make them publicly available for subscription), even if you're not friends with her.

**Tip** Subscribing to your own notes sounds weird, but it's useful if you want to package your notes for cutting and pasting to another blog service (see page 90).

- **A subscription that shows you all your notifications.** Unless you tell it differently, Facebook assumes you want to see your notifications (page 83) in the Notifications tab and in your email inbox. But if you prefer, you can choose to view them in subscription form—handy if you want to keep in touch with your Facebook pals without having to log in to the site or comb through a mountain of emails.

## Subscribing to Friends' Status Updates

1. **At the top of any Facebook screen, click the down arrow next to Friends, and then choose Status Updates.** The Status Updates tab appears, listing the current status of all your friends.

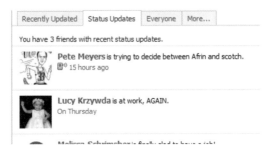

2. **Head to the right side of the Status Updates tab and click the Friends' Status Feed link.**

3. **Follow the steps on page 88.**

## Subscribing to Friends' Posts

You can sign up for one subscription that shows you all the stuff all your friends post—Web sites, video clips, and so on—or one subscription for each of the friends you're interested in. Here's how:

1. **In the Applications menu on the left side of your screen, click Posted Items (you may have to click "more" to see the Posted Items link).**

2. **On the Posted Items page that appears, head to the "Show recently posted items by" drop-down box and choose either All Friends or the name of one of your friends.**

3. **Head to the right side of the Posted Items page and click either My Friends' Posted Items (if you chose All Friends in step 2) or a link similar to "Stan Dupp's Posted Items" (if you chose a specific friend in step 2).**

Subscribe to Posted Items
My Friends' Posted Items
Subscription Help »

Posted Items Help

4. **Follow the steps on page 88.**

## Subscribing to People's Notes

Page 90 tells you all about notes (Facebook's version of blogs). To subscribe to someone's notes:

1. **In the Applications menu on the left side of your screen, click Notes (you may have to click "more" to see the Notes link).**

2. **On the Notes page that appears, click the My Friends' Notes link.**

> **Tip** To subscribe to an individual's notes, whether or not that person is your friend, surf to her profile (page 36), and then scroll down to the Notes section and click See All. Then, on the person's Notes page, click the "Eileen Doe's Notes" link (or whatever the person's name is).

3. **Follow the steps on page 88.**

# Subscribing to Your Notifications

1. **At the top of any Facebook screen, click the down arrow next to Inbox, and then choose Notifications.** Facebook displays the Notifications tab.

2. **Scroll to the bottom of the Notifications tab and click the Your Notifications link on the right-hand side.**

3. **Follow the steps below.**

# Finalizing Your Subscription

1. **No matter what kind of subscription you're signing up for, the following steps apply.** (Do them *after* you've finished the steps for the particular feed you're subscribing to.)

2. **In the page that appears, click "Subscribe to this feed" (or the similarly worded link that appears in your browser).**

3. **In the box that appears, choose the bookmark folder you want to put your subscription in.** The feed name Facebook suggests is perfectly workable, if a little boring, so don't feel you have to type in a new one (although you can if you want). Because you access subscriptions through your Web browser, the folder you choose from the "Create in" drop-down list (or create using the "New folder" button) appears in your Web browser's feeds list.

> **Note** Bookmarking a Web page makes it easy for you to return to that page again later. You see the name of your subscription's bookmark folder when you view your Web browser's feeds list. (Every browser is different. To see your feeds list on Internet Explorer, click the Favorites Center button—the tiny yellow star at the left of the main menu).

**You've successfully subscribed to this feed!**

Updated content can be viewed in Internet Explorer and other programs that use the Common Feed List.

☆ View my feeds

4. **Click Subscribe.** Up pops a message telling you your subscription was successful. To see your subscription, you can either click the "View my feeds" link on the success message, or use your browser's menu to see all your listed feeds. If you use Internet Explorer, for example, click the Favorites Center icon (the little star on the left side of the menu) to view your feeds.

 If you're not thrilled with the way your Web browser displays your subscriptions (a.k.a. feeds), you can use a free news aggregator service such as *www.Bloglines.com* to display them instead. You need a feed's URL to view it using an aggregator. If you're using Internet Explorer as your Web browser, try right-clicking your feed listing, and then choosing Properties to see the feed's copy-and-paste-able URL.

# Creating Notes (Blogs)

Ever since "blogosphere" replaced the more mundane "bunch o' personal Web sites," every site worth its salt offers free *blogs*—easy-to-use online journals where you chronicle your hobbies, family or work life, or whatever you feel like writing about. Facebook offers free blogs, too—it just calls them *notes* instead.

> **Note** There's a slight—but very important—difference between notes and regular old blogs: Because Facebook integrates notes with all the other stuff you do on the site (thanks to tagging), notes can actually document the complex social interactions between you and your friends (and your friends and *their* friends, and so on). It's scary, it's exciting, it's très 21st-century—and it's a marketer's dream come true.

You can either upload an existing blog (if you have one) into notes, or you can create your own notes from scratch. And here's the cool part: You can *tag* your notes. *Tagging* a note means associating one or more of your Facebook friends' names with the note. For example, say you write a note describing the fishing trip you and your pal Fred took together. You can tag the note with Fred's name, making it easy for Fred—and his Facebook friends—to locate your tale of the trip.

After you create a note, Facebook lists the note's subject line on your profile page (look for the Notes section) so other folks can find your note and comment on it. At the same time, the site automatically sends notifications to all the friends you tagged so they can check out what you said about them.

> **Note** By tweaking your Notes privacy settings (which you access by clicking the "Edit notes privacy" link shown on page 95), you can control who gets to know about, see, and comment on your notes. Flip to page 96 for step-by-step details.

## Typing Notes from Scratch

If you don't already have a blog, or you *do* have a blog but you don't want to cut and paste it into Facebook, you need to start fresh. To create your first blog installment on Facebook:

1. **From the Applications menu on the left side of any Facebook screen, choose Notes.**

**Note** If you don't see Notes in the Applications menu, expand the menu by scrolling to the bottom of it and clicking the "more" link.

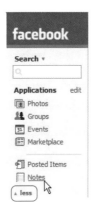

2. **On the Notes page that appears, click "Write a New Note".** On the "Write a Note" page, fill in the Title field with a subject line for your note (think of it as a summary of your entry and shoot for provocative, concise, or both). In the Body field, type your note.

☐ **Write a Note**

**Title:**

**Body:**

Feeling **bold**? Format your note.

**Photos:** No photos.

**Upload a photo:** Choose a photo from your computer to upload to this note.

[                    ] [ Browse... ]

[ Publish ]  [ Preview ]  [ Cancel ]

**Tag people in this note:**
Type any name

**In this note:**
No one.

3. **If you like, add a photo or two.** To do so, click the Browse button and, in the window that appears, select the image file you want to add. Repeat this process to add additional photos.

4. **If you want to, tag the note.** Tagging is a way of associating the note with a Facebook friend (or two). If your note chronicles the office Christmas party, say, you might want to tag the office mates you mention. To tag your note, click the "Tag people in this note" field and start typing; then choose one of the names Facebook helpfully displays.

---

**Note** For a blow-by-blow on tagging, see page 99.

---

5. **Click Preview to give your note a quick once-over.** Double-check what you've written and check the formatting, which can get a little funky (especially if you added photos). If you see something you don't like, click Edit to change your note. Then repeat the Preview–Edit cycle until you're happy with the result.

---

**Tip** Facebook uses HTML (hypertext markup language) to format notes. If you know HTML, use it: Type HTML tags directly into the Body field along with your text. To see a quick-and-dirty HTML cheatsheet, click the "Format your note" link just below the Body field. To learn more about HTML, check out *Creating Web Sites: The Missing Manual.*

6. **Click Publish.** Facebook lists your new note in the Notes section of your profile for all the world (technically, all your friends and fellow network members) to see and comment on, and sends notifications to the folks you tagged.

> **Note** After you publish your note, you can share it with people who aren't yet on Facebook. To do so: From the My Notes page (see page 95), head to the title of the note you want to share and click the Share button.

# Importing Notes from an Existing Blog

If you've already got a blog on some other site (such as *www.Typepad.com* or *www.Blogger.com*), you can tell Facebook to duplicate your blog entries as Facebook notes. That way, the people on Facebook can read your musings without your having to type every blog entry twice.

> **Note** You can't use Facebook to edit the notes you import from some other blogging site. Instead, you have to edit your notes using the other blogging service's Web site, just as you do now. Think of Facebook's version as a reprint.

To import blog entries from an existing blog into Facebook:

1. **From the Applications menu on the left side of your screen, choose Notes.** You may have to click "more" to see the Notes link.

2. **On the Notes page that appears, click My Notes, and then click "Import a blog" on the right side of the page.**

**Import an External Blog**

You can import posts from one external blog so that they appear along with your notes. Facebook will automatically update your notes whenever you write in your blog. Imported blog posts cannot be edited.

**Please only import your own blog.** If you import too many blog posts in a day, you could be blocked from writing or importing new notes, and this could result in your account being disabled.

**You are not importing from an external blog to your notes.**
Enter a URL below to import to your notes.

Web URL:    [ Enter a website or RSS/Atom feed address ]

☐ By entering a URL, you represent that you have the right to permit us to reproduce this content on the Facebook site and that the content is not obscene or illegal.

[ Start Importing ]

3. **On the "Import a Blog" page, head to the Web URL field and type in your blog's URL (for example,** *http://YourNameHere.blogspot. com*). Turn on the checkbox to reassure Facebook that the blog you're importing is yours (it needs to be; adding anything to your Facebook account that you personally haven't created or bought rights to distribute spells copyright infringement), and then click Start Importing.

This is a preview of your imported blog.

We retrieved these entries from your feed at
http://mamabearmag.blogspot.com/feeds/posts/default?alt=rss

If you confirm this import, we'll check the feed every couple of hours for new posts you've made, and add anything we find to your Facebook notes.

[ Confirm Import ]
[ Cancel ]

**Import Info:**
This is a preview of your imported blog.
You can continue to import this blog or cancel.

**Mama Bear Signs On**
11:50pm Today
This note is imported. View original post

4. **In the confirmation page that appears, click Confirm Import.** Facebook adds the imported blog entries to your from-scratch notes with one difference: a tiny orange icon that lets people know the entries have been imported from somewhere else. If folks click the "View original post" link, they'll jump to the blog the entry came from.

# Viewing and Changing Your Notes

Facebook makes it easy to see all the notes you've written and change or delete them, one at a time. To see and edit your notes:

**Note** If you import notes, you can't change them in Facebook. You can, however, see and delete them by following the steps below.

1. **From the Applications menu, choose Notes.** You may have to click "more" to see the Notes link.

2. **On the Notes page that appears, click the My Notes link in the upper left.** If you don't see the full text of your notes, click the My Notes tab.

3. **To edit your note, head to the note's title line and click Edit Note.**
4. **To delete your note, click Delete.**

# Restricting Access to Your Notes

Unless you tell Facebook otherwise, all your Facebook friends and fellow network members can see, subscribe to, and comment on the notes you write. But you can customize access to your notes so that:

- All Facebook members can see your notes.
- Only the people in certain networks (such as your work network or your school network) can see them.
- Only your friends can see them.
- Only the people you've tagged in your notes can see them.
- Only your friends can comment on your notes.
- Nobody can comment on your notes.
- Nobody can subscribe to your notes.

> **Note** For the scoop on subscriptions, see page 84.

To modify access to your notes:

1. **From the Applications menu, choose Notes.** As always, you may have to click "more" to see the Notes link.

2. **On the Notes page that appears, click My Notes in the upper left.** Then, on the My Notes tab that appears, head to the right side of the page and click "Edit notes privacy".

**Privacy Settings for Notes**

Only your friends, and everyone from Rio Grande Valley, TX, can see your notes.

Back to Profile Privacy without saving changes.

**Notes**

You can allow **all your networks** to see your notes, or you can select **restricted** settings to allow only people from certain networks and your friends to see your notes. You can also select **only me**, which means that only you and people tagged in your notes can see your notes.

    All my networks and all my friends    ▾    ├────────────┤

**Comments**

You can select who can comment on your notes.

⦿ Anyone who can see my notes can post comments

◯ Only my friends can post comments

◯ Turn comments off

**Syndication**

You can select who can subscribe to your notes.

⦿ Anyone who can see my notes can subscribe to my notes

◯ No one can subscribe

[ Save ]  [ Cancel ]

3. **Change who can access or add public comments to your notes.** From the drop-down list in the Notes section, choose the option that best describes who you want to be able to read your notes. Then head to the Comments section and tell Facebook who you want to let comment on your notes (see the next section of this book). Finally, to prevent people from subscribing to your notes, scroll down to the Syndication section and turn on the "No one can subscribe" radio button. When you finish making changes, click Save.

# Adding Comments to Notes

Every time Facebook displays a note that you (or anyone else) has created, it also displays a link people can use to comment publicly on that note.

But where to start? I figure this has to have been tried down here before, and I also figure there has to be a gardening club or two with members who know the scoop. But I'll be dogged if I've been able to track them down.

In this note: Charity Avendano (notes)

4 comments | ( Add a comment )                    Updated 19 hours ago

**Note** If you don't want people commenting on your notes, you can tell Facebook to remove the "Add a comment" link from your notes—see page 96.

Comments give the people who read your notes an easy way to stroke your ego, give you advice, or post helpful resources. And because the comments people leave appear one after the other, right after the text of your note, they're easy to see and to change. On a notes page, you can:

- **Add a comment to someone else's note.** However you stumble across someone else's note—by viewing your friends' notes (from the Applications menu, choose Notes), surfing to the Notes section of a fellow network member's profile (page 26), or perusing Popular Notes (from the Applications menu, choose Notes, and then click the Popular Notes link)—the way you add a comment is the same: Simply click the "Add a comment" link at the bottom of the note. (If you don't see this link, it's because the note writer told Facebook to remove it—see page 96.)

**Note** Unless you tell it otherwise, Facebook automatically notifies you when someone comments on one of your notes. (Page 83 tells you how to change this behavior.)

- **View the comments other people have added to your note.** From the Applications menu, choose Notes and then click the My Notes link. Then scroll down to the bottom of your note to see all the comments people have left for you.

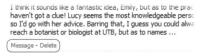

- **Delete a comment someone has added to your note.** Perhaps someone added an offensive comment, or just one you'd prefer your friends not to see. Head to the bottom of the comment and click Delete; then, in the confirmation box that appears, click Delete again.

**Note** If someone leaves an inappropriate comment—and overzealous marketing people, among others, have been known to do just that—you can send him a "cease and desist" message by clicking the Message link at the bottom of the comment. If that doesn't do the trick, you can block that person from seeing your notes (page 236) or report him to Facebook (page 237).

# Tagging Notes

Tagging a note links the note to one or more of your friends, whether or not the person's actually mentioned in the body of the note. It's a win-win situation: Your friends get warm fuzzies from being tagged (everybody likes to feel important), you get more folks reading your notes, and the companies that advertise on Facebook get a more complete picture of your social network.

You can tag a note while you're creating it—as explained on page 92—but you can also tag a note after you've published it. To do so:

1. **From the Applications menu, choose Notes.** You may have to click "more" to see the Notes link.

2. **On the Notes page that appears, click My Notes.** Make sure the My Notes tab is selected.

3. **Scroll down to just below the note's title and click the Edit Note link.**

4. **In the "Tag people in this note" field, start typing the name of the friend you want to tag.** Facebook pops up names as you type; click to select one. You can tag as many of your friends as you like.

| Edit Note | |
|---|---|
| Title: | Tag people in this note: |
| Calling all Brownsville gardeners! | Type any name |
| Body: | |
| <Photo 1> | In this note: |
| Okay, so one of my oh-so-kind neighbors invited me to join a group that's | |

5. **Scroll down to the bottom of the page and click Save.**

# Finding Mentions of Yourself in People's Notes

Just as you can tag notes with your friends' names, they can tag their notes with yours. To see a list of all your friends' notes that mention you:

1. **From the Applications menu, choose Notes.** You may have to click "more" to see the Notes link.

2. **On the Notes page that appears, click "Notes about You."** All the notes your friends have tagged with your name appear.

> **Note** You would never write a note describing a scene of wild debauchery and then tag a squeaky-clean, trying-to-land-an-important-job friend (thus ruining any chance she has of passing her pre-interview background check). But some people would. Fortunately, Facebook lets you delete tags, even if someone else added them. On the Notes About Me tab, scroll down to the note you want to disassociate yourself from and click the "remove tag" link that appears just under your name.

# Controlling What People See About You

As part of its mission to provide as much customizable privacy as possible, Facebook lets you prevent people from subscribing to your notes and to your status updates. You can also remove certain details about your actions from your mini-feed and from the news feeds your friends receive.

## Preventing People from Subscribing to Your Notes

If you don't want to let anyone subscribe to your notes (page 87), follow these steps:

1. **In the Applications menu on the right side of your screen, click Notes (you may have to click "more" to see the Notes link).**

2. **On the right-hand side of the Notes page that appears, under the Notes Settings heading, click the "Edit notes privacy" link.**

3. **On the Privacy Settings for Notes page, head down to the Syndication section and turn on the "No one can subscribe" radio button.**

# Preventing People from Subscribing to Your Status Updates

If you don't want people to instantly know when you change your status from "Hard at work" to "Counting the seconds till quittin' time," here's what you do:

1. **On the Facebook main menu, click "privacy"; then, from the Privacy Overview page that appears, choose Profile.**

2. **On the "Privacy Settings for your Profile" page, turn off the checkbox next to "Allow friends to subscribe to my status updates".**

# Removing Details from Your Mini-feed

Here's how to tell Facebook which of your activities it can automatically tell your friends about via their news feeds or your mini-feed—and which it can't:

1. **On the Facebook main menu, click "privacy".**

2. **In the Privacy Overview page that appears, click "News Feed and Mini-Feed".** Up pops the "News Feed and Mini-Feed Privacy" page.

**News Feed and Mini-Feed Privacy**
Back to Privacy Overview without saving changes.

Facebook will only publish stories about you on your Mini-Feed and in the News Feeds of your friends.

Stories are published when you edit your profile information, join a new network, or update your Status. Also publish stories when you...

- ☐ Remove Profile Info
- ☑ Write a Wall Post
- ☐ Comment on a Note
- ☑ Comment on a Photo
- ☑ Comment on a Video
- ☑ Comment on a Posted Item
- ☐ Post on a Discussion Board
- ☐ Add a Friend
- ☑ Remove my Relationship Status
- ☐ Leave a Group
- ☑ Leave a Network

Have something you'd like to see here?

Mini-Feed can show the time when stories were published.

- ☑ Show times in my Mini-Feed

[ Save Changes ]  [ Cancel ]

3. **Turn off the checkboxes next to the activities you don't want to advertise.** When you're done, click Save Changes.

# Participating in Groups

One of Facebook's most popular features is *groups*—collections of people who share interests. Some groups exist only online, but some real-world groups use Facebook to keep in touch. If you want to find other folks who share a passion for just about anything from Abraham Lincoln to shoe shopping, Facebook can help. And if it turns out you can't find a group devoted to something you love, you can always create one. This chapter shows you how to find, join, and participate in groups—and how to start your own.

# What's a Group?

A Facebook *group* is a handful (or more) of members who share a passion: knitting, parenting, coding Facebook applications, collecting Beanie Babies, whatever. Groups help people share information, tips, and advice. And they're not just virtual: Lots of groups that meet in person use Facebook groups to keep in touch between meetings.

> **Note** Group-related events make it super easy for Facebook members to meet in person; see Chapter 7 for details.

Whoever starts a group gets to decide who can join. Some groups let anyone join; some let all Facebook members apply, but then choose who can join; and some groups hide their activities from everyone but group members. Once you're a member of a group, you get to do things like post messages and pictures on the group bulletin board, create and attend group-related events, and more.

> **Note** Technically, Groups is a Facebook *application* (page 206), so it's not a built-in part of Facebook. Chances are you'll never care about this distinction *unless* you decide to replace Groups with another application (see Chapter 12).

Because groups are easy to start and join, there are zillions of them. So, along with the social-, craft-, business-, and sports-related groups, you find a lot of silly groups like "People Against Wet Cheetos," "I Judge People Who Use Poor Grammar," and "If 500,000 People Join This Group I Will Change My Middle Name to Facebook."

Fortunately, Facebook gives you a couple of tools—explained next—to separate the wheat from the chaff and find a group you'll benefit from and enjoy. And if you can't find such a group, you can create your own.

> **Note** Unless you tell Facebook otherwise (page 224), everyone who can see your profile can also see which groups you've joined. Some people use group membership as a way to express their personal and political views. Join a group called "Vote No on Proposition 100" or "People for the Ethical Treatment of Corporations," for example, and people scanning your profile will draw their own conclusions.

# Finding Existing Groups

Facebook gives you three ways to search for groups you'd like to join:

- **Browse based on a handful of criteria.** Unless you know the name or subject of the group you're looking for (in which case, try the next option), this is the quickest way to find a group.

- **Search for specific groups and topics.** If your buddy told you the name of a group you want to join or if you're interested only in groups devoted to a specific subject—like the music of Todd Rundgren—this is your quickest option.

- **View the most popular groups on the site.** Finding out which groups your fellow network members have joined during the last 24 hours is interesting, even if you decide not to follow their lead.

> **Note** Another way to join a Facebook group is to respond to an invitation sent by another member (see page 113).

## Browsing for Groups

*Browsing* lets you see a listing of all the groups associated with a particular network—for example, only groups created by people who live in your area—and a particular category, such as food & drink, self-help, and so on. To browse for groups:

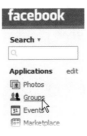

1. **In the Applications menu on the left side of the Facebook main menu, click Groups.** The left side of the Groups page that appears shows you what groups your friends have joined, which can be interesting; the right side shows the groups you've already joined.

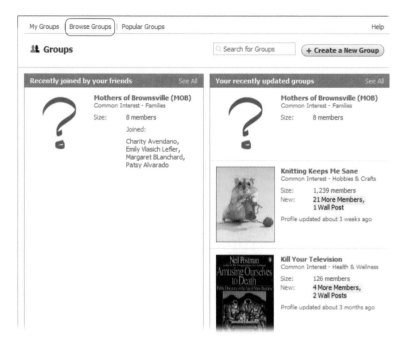

2. **On the Groups page, click Browse Groups.**

3. **On the Browse Groups page, choose the categories you want to browse.** Group listings appear on the left side of the page, beginning with any groups you've already joined, followed by groups Facebook thinks you might be interested in joining (based on profile information such as the networks you're in) and then by all the rest of the groups you can join. You can:

   — **Scroll through the humongous list of groups a page at a time.** Drag your browser screen's slider to see all the groups on the first page; click Next (or a page number) to view another pageful of results. If you've got time to kill, scrolling through these groups can be pretty entertaining. But if you're in a hurry, you'll want to filter the groups.

   — **Filter the groups.** To see only groups associated with one of your networks—useful if you're looking for local or work-related groups—choose a network from the Network drop-down list on the right. To see only those groups that have to do with business, music, sports, or some other broad topic, choose a type from the Type drop-down list. You can click one of the Subtypes (which change based on the Type you select) to further narrow your results.

## 👥 Browse Groups

( **+ Create a New Group** )

Displaying groups 1 - 10 out of over 500.

[ **1** 2 3 Next ]

| | | | |
|---|---|---|---|
| Group: | **Knitting Keeps Me Sane** | View Group | |
| Network: | Global | | |
| Size: | 1,240 members | | |
| Type: | Common Interest - Hobbies & Crafts | | |
| New: | 22 More Members, 1 Wall Post | | |

| | | | |
|---|---|---|---|
| Group: | **Kill Your Television** | ( View Group ) | |
| Network: | Global | | |
| Size: | 126 members | | |
| Type: | Common Interest - Health & Wellness | | |
| New: | 4 More Members, 2 Wall Posts | | |

| | | |
|---|---|---|
| Group: | **Mothers of Brownsville (MOB)** | View Group |

**Filter groups by:**

**Network**
My Networks ▼

**Type**
Common Interest ▼

( Subtype )
**All**
Activities
Age
Beauty
Beliefs & Causes
Current Events
Dating & Relationships
Families
Food & Drink
Friends
Gardening
Health & Wellness
History
Hobbies & Crafts
Languages
Pets & Animals

4. **To learn more about a group, click either the group's name or the View Group link next to it.** Up pops the group's profile page with info you can use to decide whether you want to join this group. You can check out the group's discussion board, see the pictures people have posted, or see what's written on the group's wall.

---

**Kill Your Television**                                          Global

**Information**

**Group Info**

Name:         Kill Your Television
Type:         Common Interest - Health & Wellness
Description:  This is a group dedicated to countering a television saturated society and discussing the effects of the triviality it has brought upon our society.

According to the late Neil Postman in "Amusing Ourselves to Death," the transition in our culture from print-based communication to television-based communication has brought with it a glut of social ills. This trivial television culture has birthed staggering intellectual laziness that is resistant to intelligent and profitable information and discussion. The tragedy of this societal shift is that society has embraced this new epistemology uncritically and unaware. We are, to use Postman's own words, amusing ourselves to death.

I ask that those who join this group not watch more than 5 hours of TV (movies are different... that could be a great discussion) a week. Or if you tourture yourself with such veiwing and are trying to cut it down and are at least disgusted with the fact that you have bound yourself with the chains of triviality, then I guess you can join also. What a waste of 5 hours anyway, but hey

( View Discussion Board )
Join this Group

[ Share + ]

**Related Groups**

Congressman Ron Paul for President 2008
Student Groups - Political Groups

The Largest Facebook Group Ever
Just for Fun - Facebook Classics

Calvinism: The Group That Chooses You

# Searching for Groups

If you know the name of the group you're looking for or you're interested only in groups whose names include a certain word, searching is the way to go. To search for groups:

1. **From the Applications menu, choose Groups.**

2. **In the search box that appears, type the word (or words) you want to search group titles for and hit Return.** If you get too many results, you can winnow them down by choosing a network from the All Networks drop-down list or by clicking Filter Results, which lets you choose a Type and a Subtype as shown on page 107.

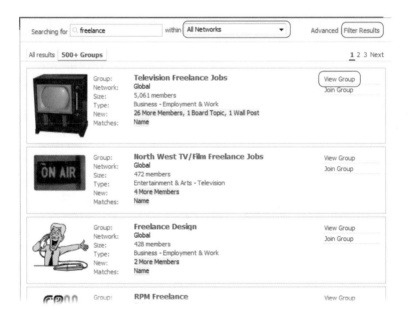

3. **When you spot a listing you're interested in, click either the group's name, or the group's View Group link.** Facebook displays the group's profile page so you can learn more about the group.

## Finding Popular Groups

Everybody likes to know what's hot. There's a good chance you won't actually want to *join* a group just because everybody else is doing it, but taking a peek at what's popular can be a fun way to kill a couple of minutes. To see which groups the people in your networks have joined in the past 24 hours, from the Applications menu, choose Groups, and then click the Popular Groups link.

# Joining a Group

Facebook lets you join up to 200 groups, so you can join one group for each of your diverse interests—and a few just for fun. To join a group:

1. **Go to either the listing (page 108) or profile page (page 107) of the group you want to join.**

2. **Click Join Group or Join this Group, respectively.**

3. **In the confirmation box that appears, click Join.** If the group is *open* (page 111), that's it—you're in. If the group's by invitation only, Facebook sends your request to the group administrator, and you have to wait for approval.

> **Note** If a group is *closed* (page 112), you can't just join—you have to be invited *and* approved. You know a group is closed if you don't see the Join Group link in the group's listing. Instead, on the group's profile page, you see a "Request to Join Group" link. Click it to send the group's administrator a message requesting an invitation to join. If the administrator decides to approve your request, you'll get a Facebook notification telling you so.

After you've joined a group, head to the Applications menu and click Groups, and you'll see your new group listed on the Groups page. All the groups you've joined appear in the Groups section of your profile, too.

# Creating a Group

If you scan through all the groups on Facebook and can't find one that fits your needs, no problem—just start your own.

**Note** You can create *almost* any group that you can dream up. In its terms of use fine print, Facebook reserves the right to pull the plug on hate groups and other unsavories—and it has. If you come across a candidate for plug-pulling, you can send a heads-up to Facebook's customer service team by scrolling down to the bottom of the group's profile page and clicking Report Group.

To start your own group:

1. **From the Applications menu, choose Groups.**

2. **On the right-hand side of the Groups page, click "Create a New Group".**

3. **On the "Step 1: Group Info" tab, fill in the text fields.** You have to fill out some fields—like Group Name, Network (the network whose members you want to join your group), and Group Type (such as business or sports)—while others are optional. More is better: Details make it easier for prospective members to understand the purpose of the group, and make it more likely that you'll attract the kind of people you're looking for.

4. **If you want an egalitarian group that anyone can join, leave the "This group is open" radio button turned on; scroll to the bottom of the page and click Create Group.** Otherwise, you'll want to turn off some or all of the features. For example, say you're creating a work-related group to keep your clients up-to-date on one of your projects. In this case, you want a private, all-information-flows-one-way group; to make that happen, turn off all the Enable radio boxes, switch access to "This group is secret", and turn off the Publicize checkbox. After you've made your selections, click Create Group.

5. **In the "Step 2: Picture" tab that appears, upload a photo, if you like.** Click Browse to find an image file on your computer that you want to associate with your group, such as a photo, drawing, or logo. When you've found it, turn on the checkbox that protects Facebook from any media piracy on your part, and then click Upload Picture.

**⚇ Create a Group**

Step 1: Group Info | Step 2: Picture | Step 3: Members

**Your group has been created.**

**Current Picture**

?

**Upload Picture**

You can upload a JPG, GIF or PNG file.

[ Browse... ]

☐ I certify that I have the right to distribute this picture
and that it does not violate the Terms of Use.

[ Upload Picture ] [ Skip for Now ]

File size limit 4 MB. If your upload does not work, try a smaller picture.

6. **In the "Step 3: Members" tab, invite a few friends to join your group, and then click "Finish and View".** You can type both names of your Facebook friends and email addresses of people who aren't on Facebook yet. (Non-Facebook members can see the group but can't join it until they join Facebook.) After you click "Finish and View", Facebook shows you the profile page for your new group, complete with administrator-level features (like Message All Members, Edit Group, and Create Related Event—see page 116) that only you can see.

View Discussion Board
Message All Members
Edit Group
Edit Members
Edit Group Officers
Invite People to Join
edit  Create Related Event
Leave Group

Share +

Events We're Hosting

# Inviting People to Join A Group

If you're starting a group, you can invite people to join during the creation process (page 112). But you can also do so after the fact—and so can other group members.

> **Note** If the person who created a group made it part of the *Global network* (page 27), then any Facebook member can join. If a group's limited to a specific network, then only network members can join.

To invite someone to join a group:

1. **Head to the group's profile page (page 107) and click the "Invite People to Join" link on the right-hand side.**

2. **On the page that appears, type the names of the Facebook friends you want to invite, or the email addresses of people not on Facebook yet.** To invite Facebook friends, you can either turn on the checkbox next to a friend's name (Facebook lists all of your friends who are eligible to join based on the group's network settings), or head down to the "Invite People who are not on Facebook via Email" field and type in a bunch of email addresses separated by commas. (Non-Facebook members can see details about the group but can't join it until they join Facebook.)

> **Note** If you have a really big social circle, you might want to avoid paging through a bazillion checkboxes as you hunt for that certain someone to invite. Instead, click in the "Invite Friends on Facebook" field and type the name of the friend you want to invite or Friend List you previously created (page 51).

## Deleting a Group You Started

Sometimes you goof or change your mind. If you started a group but a couple minutes later decide it wasn't such a great idea, you can delete it. Here's how:

> **Note** You can only delete a group that you started. What's more, as soon as somebody else joins your group, Facebook yanks your ability to delete it. What you *can* do at that point is step down as administrator. (When you do, Facebook offers the gig to the remaining members of the group.) You follow the same steps listed below to delete a group or to step down as administrator.

1. **On the group's profile page (page 107), choose Leave Group.** If you're the one-and-only member of a group, leaving the group tells Facebook to delete it. If you're not the one-and-only member, leaving the group means the group still exists without you in it.

2. **In the confirmation box that appears, click Remove.**

# Participating in Groups

As you saw on page 111, group creators get to pick and choose which privileges they want members to have. So the things you get to do as a group member depend on how the group was set up. (Group *creators* always get carte blanche.)

## If You're a Group Member

As a group member, you *may* get to:

- **Add photos, videos, and links to the group's profile page.** To add photos or video clips, surf to the group's profile page (page 107), and then click Add Photos or Add Videos. To add a link to a Web site, type the link into the "Post a link" field, and then click Post.

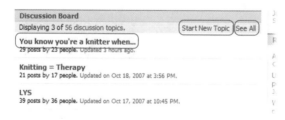

- **Participate in the discussion board that appears on the group's profile page.** On the group's profile page, scroll down until you see the Discussion Board section. There, you can:

  — **Click a subject line** to display the entire post (followed by the pre-ceding posts in that discussion thread), along with links you can use to reply to the post on the board (Reply to Post) or send a per-sonal message to the poster (Send Message).

  — **Click Start New Topic** to show a tab you can use to start your very own discussion thread.

  — **Click See All** to see the whole discussion board, not just the snip-pet that fits on the group's profile page.

- **Write on the group's wall.** Scroll down to the Wall section of the group's profile page, and then click Write Something.

- **Invite people to join the group.** On the group's profile page, click the "Invite People to Join" link (see page 113).

- **Leave the group.** On the group's profile page, click the Leave Group link.

## If You're the Group Creator

Group creators can do everything members can do, plus:

- **Send a message to all group members all at once.** On the group's profile page, click Message All Members. Up pops the Compose Message tab, pre-filled with the name of your group.

> **Note:** If your group's membership tops 1,000, you're out of luck: The Message All Members feature won't work. This is part of Facebook's effort to stop spam.

- **Create a group-related event.** A *group-related event* is an *event* (page 119) that shows up on the group's profile page. When you set up a group-related event, Facebook automatically sends an invitation to all group members. To create such an event: On the group's profile page, click the Create Related Event link, and then follow the steps on page 127.

- **Administer the group.** Facebook lets you change the way your group works. Among other things, you can disable the group's wall or discussion board, delete members, and grant members *officer* (feel-good title) or *administrator* (actual power) status. On the group's profile page, click Edit Group to change what appears on the Group Info tab (page 111), Edit Members to invite members as shown on page 113, or Edit Group Officers to share your administrative powers with another group member.

# Facebook and the Real World: In-person Events

**C**onnecting with online pals in the real world is becoming more and more popular. Facebook's event listings help you find out what's going on in your own backyard—everything from birthday parties and gallery openings to study sessions and protest marches. And because RSVPing to events lets your Facebook friends see that you're planning to attend, a tiny get-together can quickly burgeon ("Well, hey, if Bob and Muffy are going, then *I'm* going!"). This chapter shows you how to find out what events are happening in your area, who's attending, and how to set up your own events.

# The Three Different Kinds of Events

Face-to-face raises privacy issues that don't exist online. As creepy as someone might be online (leaving weird or threatening notes on your wall, poking you a hundred times a day, or joining every group you join), the worst risks you take are annoyance, embarrassment, and the possible filching of some personal data, all of which Chapter 13 helps you prevent. In person, though, that same creepiness could conceivably translate into actual bodily harm. So be extremely careful if you arrange a real-life meeting with someone (or a group of people) you met on Facebook.

To help deal with the privacy issues and safety concerns raised by in-person events, Facebook offers these event types:

- **Open events.** Any Facebook member can read about an open event on the event's profile page and add himself to the guest list. Open events are great for festivals, concerts, and other get-togethers held in public venues. You know an event is open by the "Add to My Events" link on the search listing description for the event (page 122), and by the "This is an open event" message on the Event Type section of the event's profile.

- **Closed events.** Any Facebook member can see a description of the event on the event's profile page, but nobody gets on the guest list without an invitation. Anyone can *request* an invitation, but the event's administrator gets the final say. Closed events are perfect for club and school meetings. You know an event is closed when you see the Request Invitation link (or the "closed" description) on the event's profile.

- **Secret events.** Only those people who receive an invitation (either via Facebook notification or email) can tell that the event exists. Use this kind of event when you're planning a business meeting, private party, or intergalatic invasion.

**Note** The *event administrator*—the person who dreams up the event, adds it to Facebook, and manages the guest list—gets to decide what kind of event it is.

# Finding Existing Events

Facebook gives you four different ways to find events you might want to attend:

- **Search for events by name or subject.** You can find events using the same search box you use to look up Facebook members (page 36).

- **Browse for events.** Browsing lets you look at all the events scheduled during a specific time period, related to a certain network, or held for a particular reason. For example, you can find all the political rallies planned for your town in the next week.

- **Check out the events your friends plan to attend.** There's a good chance you'll be interested in the activities your friends enjoy.

- **Take a peek at the most popular events.** You can see a list of the hottest events in your networks based on RSVP activity in the past 24 hours.

## Searching for Events by Name or Subject

If you know the name or subject of the event you're looking for—or at least a word or two of the name or subject—the easiest way to find it is to search for it directly.

**Note** It probably goes without saying, but for you to be able to look up a karate-related event, the event's creator had to put the word *karate* in the name of the event or somewhere in the description.

To do so:

1. **In the Search box just above the Applications menu, type the name of an event or words you want to search for, and then hit Return.**

**Note** You can also search for events using the search box on the Events page. To get there, click Events in the Applications menu.

2. **On the search results page that appears, click the Events tab.** Doing so filters out all the non-event results.

3. **Click the name of an event to see its profile page.** Alternatively, you can click the View Event link. Either way, the page that appears describes the event in detail and lists confirmed and possible attendees (scroll down to see all the particulars).

# Browsing for Events

When you browse, at first you get a list of *all* the events scheduled on Facebook, but you can narrow your focus to events based on a bunch of criteria. Here's how:

1. **From the Applications menu, choose Events.** Up pops the Events page, with Upcoming Events tab displayed. If you've RSVPed to any events, they show up here.

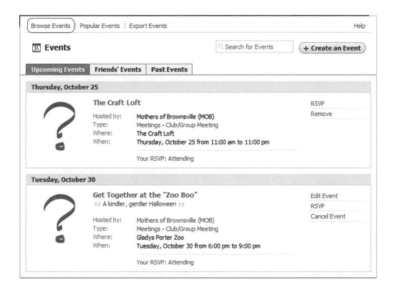

2. **Click Browse Events.** The Browse Events page that appears lists all the events in the next 30 days that are associated with your networks. (When you create an event—see page 126—you have to link it with a network.)

> **Note** Facebook doesn't automatically show you events associated with the Global network, although you can look up these events (see page 124). Global events are a special breed: Because they aren't tied to any particular place, they're no good for scheduling face-to-face meetings. People use them for things like everybody-beam-good-thoughts-together-at-midnight meetings, political announcements, and call-in Internet radio shows.

📅 **Browse Events**                                        ( + Create a New Event )

Searching events that occur from **Today, October 23** to **Friday, November 23, 2007**.

Displaying all 10 events.

| | Event: | The Craft Loft | View Event |
|---|---|---|---|
| ? | Network: | Rio Grande Valley, TX | |
| | Type: | Meetings - Club/Group Meeting | |
| | Host: | Mothers of Brownsville (MOB) | |
| | When: | 11:00am Thursday, October 25 | |
| | Where: | The Craft Loft | |

**October 2007**

| Sun | Mon | Tue | Wed | Thu | Fri | Sat |
|---|---|---|---|---|---|---|
| | 1 | 2 | 3 | 4 | 5 | 6 |
| 7 | 8 | 9 | 10 | 11 | 12 | 13 |
| 14 | 15 | 16 | 17 | 18 | 19 | 20 |
| 21 | 22 | 23 | 24 | 25 | 26 | 27 |
| 28 | 29 | 30 | 31 | 1 | 2 | 3 |

next »

| | Event: | Harvey's 25th Bday/Costume Party | View Event |
|---|---|---|---|
| | Network: | Rio Grande Valley, TX | |
| | Type: | Party - Birthday Party | |
| | Host: | Me | |
| | When: | 10:00pm Friday, October 26 | |

**Filter events by:**

Network
| All My Networks ▾ |

Date
| One Month ▾ |

Type
| All Types ▾ |

| American Diabetes Association. | Event: | American Diabetes Walk | View Event |
|---|---|---|---|
| | Network: | Rio Grande Valley, TX | Add to My Events |
| | Type: | Causes - Fundraiser | |
| | Host: | Lisa Killion | |
| | When: | 7:30am Saturday, October 27 | |
| | Where: | Edinburg Children's Hospital | |

All Types
Party
Causes
Education
Meetings
Music/Arts
Sports
Trips
Other

| | Event: | Find the lost geocache | View Event |
|---|---|---|---|
| ? | Network: | Rio Grande Valley, TX | View Host Group |
| | Type: | Trips - Daytrip | Add to My Events |
| | Host: | The Canyon | |

3. **Narrow your search.** You can:

- **See events scheduled for a particular day** by clicking any shaded day on the calendar. (Unshaded days don't have any events scheduled.)

- **See events associated with a network** (including the Global network) by choosing it from the Network drop-down list.

- **See all the events during the week or month ahead** by choosing one of the options from the Date drop-down list.

- **See only certain types of events**—like parties, meetings, or school-related functions—by choosing from the Type drop-down list.

# Seeing Your Friends' Events

Checking out the events your friends are going to can be illuminating. ("Ralph's into cross-stitch? No *way!*") It might also turn up events that *you're* interested in attending. Here's how: From the Applications menu, choose Events. Then, on the Events page that appears, click the Friends' Events tab.

## Checking Out Popular Events

You can find out which events in your networks (and on the Global network) have gotten the most RSVPs in the last 24 hours by heading to the Applications menu, choosing Events, and then clicking the Popular Events link.

# RSVPing to an Event

Sure, you could show up at an event without RSVPing first, but that would be rude! It would also mean that you'd miss out on the social networking benefits Facebook offers, because as soon as you RSVP, all your friends can see where you're headed—which may encourage them to join in the fun.

**Note** Depending on how the event's administrator set up the event, other folks in the network associated with the event will be able to see that you're planning to attend (see page 127).

There are two ways to RSVP to an event:

- **If you received an invitation,** simply respond to it by following the instructions in the email or Facebook notification. You can be invited to any kind of event (open, closed, or secret), but the *only* way to RSVP to a secret event is by responding to an invitation, since you wouldn't even know about the event if you hadn't been invited.

**Note** To finagle an invitation to a closed event, click the Contact Information link on the event's profile page to send the event's administrator a polite email request.

- **If you weren't explicitly invited,** head either to the event's listing (page 124) or its profile page (page 122) and click "Add to My Events". If the event is open, you're in. Facebook updates the event's profile page to show that you're a confirmed guest, and gives you new options you can use to change your response (to "maybe" if your plans change, for example) or to invite other people. Facebook also adds the event to the Upcoming Events tab of your Events page (which you can see by heading to the Applications menu and clicking Events).

# Creating Your Own Events

Whether you want to host a product launch party, start a study group at the local coffee shop, or have a community meeting, it's easy to set up your own events on Facebook.

**Tip** If an event is closely tied to a Facebook group you created or that you've been made administrator of—say you want to set up a monthly face-to-face meeting of your book club, for example—you'll want to head to your group's profile page (page 107), click Create Related Event, and then follow steps 2–6 below. Doing so tells Facebook that your group is hosting the event and lets you invite all the group's members in one fell swoop by clicking the Invite Members button that appears on the "Step 3: Guest List" tab (see step 7).

Here's what you do:

1. **From the Applications menu, choose Events.**

2. **On the Events page that appears, click "Create an Event".**

3. **On the "Step 1: Event Info" tab, fill out as many of the fields as possible.** Some fields—like the event's name, the network you want to associate it with, and the time and location—are required, but you should fill in as many of the fields as you can. Doing so makes events easier for people to find, because they can search on every word you add. It also encourages people to RSVP, since the more people know about an event (and the better you make it sound, of course), the more likely they are to attend.

> **Tip** If you fill in the Street and City/Town fields, Facebook displays a helpful map on your event's profile page.

4. **Decide how open you want your event to be.** Facebook assumes you want an open event that everyone on the site can view and attend, and that all attendees can contribute to by uploading photos, videos, links, and wall posts. If that's fine with you—for example, if your event is one that's open to the public and is listed in the local newspapers, or is an "attend in spirit only" kind of event—you don't have to do a thing. Otherwise, you need to tweak your event's options by turning off checkboxes and turning on radio buttons. The descriptions next to each option give you a pretty clear idea of what each one does.

For most face-to-face events, you'll want to choose "This event is closed" so you don't get a bunch of riffraff showing up. If you have a very specific, finite guest list and the event is private (such as a business meeting or intimate birthday gathering), choose "This event is secret"; that way, you can invite just the folks on your list and not have to worry about strangers requesting invitations.

Don't obsess about which settings to choose for your event. You can always change them later by clicking the Edit Event link on your event's profile (page 123).

5. **Click Create Event.** Facebook posts a bare-bones version of your event on the site that people can find in searches.

6. **On the "Step 2: Picture" tab that appears, browse for the image file you want to appear on your event listing, and then click Upload Picture.** Technically, this step is optional, but a clever photo, drawing, or logo will make your event listing a lot more appealing. If you don't want to upload a picture, click "Skip for Now".

7. **Invite some guests.** Facebook lists your friends and Friend Lists (page 52) on the "Step 3: Guest List" tab that pops up, so all you need to do to invite them is choose who you want to invite and then click Add.

**Note** Facebook events are supposed to be for your friends (or for the members of groups you're in charge of—see page 116). So you can't invite Facebook members to events unless they're your friends—but you *can* invite pals who aren't yet Facebook members. To do so, on the Guest List tab, head to the "Invite People who are not on Facebook via Email" text field and type in email addresses separated by commas, and then click Add.

# 8

# Going Shopping

**A**s part of its quest to be the only Web site you'll ever need to visit, Facebook offers its very own online classified ads: Facebook Marketplace. The Marketplace ads you can see depend on the networks you belong to. And—unlike the classifieds in your local paper or ads on Craigslist.org—you can use Facebook to learn about the person who placed the ad *before* you contact him. As you'll see in this chapter, you can use Facebook Marketplace to buy or sell just about anything.

> **Note** Marketplace is a relatively new Facebook feature, so it's not quite the seller-packed, go-to shopping haunt that Craigslist is—*yet*. (Some pundits predict it never will be.) What it *is* spectacularly useful for is facilitating local sales: those Chihuahua puppies you want to get rid of, those textbooks gathering dust in the corner, that on-campus job you want to fill. Anything of special interest to your friends or fellow network members is a prime candidate for Marketplace.

# The Facebook Marketplace

Facebook's *Marketplace* is a built-in Facebook *application* (page 206) that lets you post and answer want ads. You can use Marketplace to advertise that you want to rent a house or sell a sofa—anything you're either looking for or looking to get rid of.

Because you get to choose which networks to advertise in when you place a Marketplace ad (Facebook calls them *listings*), the ads you see are ones you're most likely to want to respond to. In other words, if you browse through all the Marketplace ads associated with the San Francisco network, you won't see ads for garage sales in New York.

> **Note** Marketplace doesn't accept ads for illegal or distasteful stuff like illegal drugs, explosives, or hate-group paraphernalia. You can see the list of banned items by heading to the Applications menu, clicking Marketplace, clicking the Help link that appears on the Marketplace Home page, and then clicking the "here" link in "Click here to view the Marketplace guidelines." (You get a chance to peruse the guidelines when you create a listing—see page 136.)

| Marketplace Home | My Listings | My Friends' Listings | Add a new listing | | Help |
| --- | --- | --- | --- | --- | --- |

**Phoenix, AZ Marketplace**     Search Marketplace   For Sale ▼

| Rio Grande Valley, TX | Phoenix, AZ | < Drop | Change... |
| --- | --- | --- | --- |

| For Sale (924) | Item Wanted (74) | + **Add a new listing** |
| Housing (333) | Housing Wanted (9) | + **List what you want** |
| Jobs (240) | Looking for Work (9) | |
| Other (114) | Other Wanted (4) | |
| Free Stuff (75) | show all | |

Today

$919 - Distinctive Three Bedroom Apartment...

Sponsored Listings

Amazing deals on

## The Friend Filter: Ads from Network Connections

Thanks to the social networking information it tracks (who's friends with whom), Facebook takes the concept of personal ads a step further than your average classifieds section or even the uber-popular free listing site *Craigslist.org*. On Facebook Marketplace you can:

- **Search through just your friends' listings.** Given a choice, most people would rather do business with friends than strangers. Facebook gives you two ways of doing just that: the Marketplace page's My Friends' Listings link (page 139), and the Marketplace section of your friends' profile pages (page 6).

- **Feel out a seller by seeing the friends you have in common**. Sure, the "roommate wanted" ad sounds good, but before you contact the guy, wouldn't it be nice to contact a couple of mutual friends and find out what he's really like? (See page 140.)

> **Tip** Because its strength is putting a friendly face on ads, Facebook Marketplace is a great place to post ads you wouldn't want to put in the newspaper; for example, "Wanted: Help Moving" or "Wanted: Someone to feed my parrot while I'm on vacation."

## Cost: Free, Risk: Yours

For now, Marketplace is fee free: There's no charge for placing a regular ad or answering one. (But you can pay for special attention-getting placement of your ads; see page 136.) When you answer an ad, it's your responsibility to contact the seller and work out payment arrangements—Facebook isn't involved. So be careful: If you pay someone for his beer stein collection but he takes the money and runs, Facebook won't help get your money back.

# Placing an Ad

How you place an ad depends on whether you're listing something you have and want to sell, rent, or otherwise get rid of, or something you want. This section shows you how to do both.

## Getting Rid of Something

To place an ad for something you want to sell, rent, or give away:

1. **On the Applications menu, click Marketplace.**

2. **On the Marketplace Home page that appears, click the "Add a new listing" button.** Up pops the Marketplace Listing page.

3. **Select the category that best describes what you have to offer.**
Your options are For Sale, Housing, Jobs, Free Stuff, and Other. When
you click one of those categories, you'll see subcategories pop up.
(For example, if you click For Sale, you'll see the subcategories Books,
Furniture, Tickets, Electronics, Cars, and Other.) If you're not sure what
kind of listing belongs in a certain category or subcategory, click the
"sample" link for an example. Keep clicking, narrowing down your item
until a listing form appears with fields for the name of your item, a description, and other details.

4. **Fill out the listing form, and then click Create Listing.** The fields you see depend on what you're listing. For example, you don't see a price field if you're listing Free Stuff, and you don't see Hours or Compensation unless you're listing a job.

> **Note** Privacy-wise, Facebook doesn't treat Marketplace listings the same way it treats your profile information. If you've blocked certain Facebook members from sending you messages (see page 236), they can still contact you by responding to your listing. Bottom line? Assume everybody on the Internet can see your Marketplace listing and be careful about including sensitive info such as your phone number or home address.

There are five fields that you want to pay particular attention to (they appear on every listing form):

- **Profile.** Leave this checkbox turned on unless you don't want your listing displayed on your profile page (say you're a 300-pound bodybuilder selling a Barbie doll collection). Leaving this checkbox turned on doesn't compromise your profile information; people who can't otherwise see your profile information still won't be able to see it.

> **Tip** One good reason for leaving the profile checkbox turned on: impulse buying. Someone who found your profile because you share an affinity for ice hockey may well be interested in the skates you have for sale—even if he wasn't officially in the market for skates and so never would have found your listing in the Marketplace.

- **List Where**. Facebook automatically selects all the networks you belong to. If you don't want your ad to run in a particular network, turn off the checkbox next to it. In most cases, you want to run your listing in all the networks you belong to, to improve your chances of selling your item. (The number after the network's name is the number of network members.)

- **Privacy.** If what you're selling isn't tied to a specific network— you're not selling a textbook used only in your school, for example—you want to keep this checkbox turned on.

- **Photos.** Pictures help sell stuff, so add at least one if you can. (Facebook lets you add several.)

- **Marketplace Guidelines.** Okay, technically, this isn't a field—it's a link. Click it if you have any questions about Facebook's policies for accepting ads. In a nutshell, you have to own the stuff you're trying to sell; you can't hawk illegal, hazardous, or otherwise unsavory items; and you can't sue Facebook if you buy a lemon. Read through the guidelines at least once just so you know what you're agreeing to when you click that Create Listing button.

5. **Decide how (or if) you want to call extra attention to your listing.** After you click Create Listing, Facebook adds your listing to the Marketplace, and anyone in any of the networks you chose (and outside of those networks, too, if you left the Privacy checkbox shown on page 134 turned on) can view your listing.

   In addition, Facebook displays a "Promote your listing with a Facebook ad" link. Clicking it lets you drive traffic to your listing either by creating a *social ad* (think display ad that's targeted to a specific group of Facebook members) or a *Page* (a special kind of profile for bands, celebrities, businesses, and nonprofits). Check out Chapter 13 for the scoop on both of these options.

> **Your listing has been created.**
> It will appear in the Marketplace shortly. ( Promote your listing with a Facebook Ad. )

# Want Ads

Here's how to place an ad for an item, job, or situation that you'd like to find (like rideshare or a roommate):

1. **In the Applications menu, click Marketplace.**

2. **On the Marketplace Home page that appears, click the "List what you want" button.** Up pops the Marketplace Wanted page.

3. **Select the category that best describes what you're looking for.** Your choices are Item Wanted, Housing Wanted, Looking for Work, and Other Wanted. When you click one of those categories, you'll see subcategories pop up. Keep clicking the appropriate subcategories until a form appears with fields for the name of what you're looking for, a description, and other details.

4. **Follow steps 4–5 on page 135.** The rest of the process is identical to placing an ad for something you want to get rid of.

## Changing Your Ad

You place a Marketplace ad and then it hits you: You forgot to add an important detail. No problem! Facebook makes it easy to:

- **See your own listing.** To see a listing you've created, in the Applications menu, click Marketplace; then, on the Marketplace Home page, click My Listings. To see all the details of a listing, scroll down the My Listings page and click the listing's name.

- **Edit your listing.** You can change your ad any time: On the My Listings page (click Marketplace in the Applications menu, and then click the My Listings link), scroll down to the ad you want to change and click Edit. On the Edit Listing page that appears, make your changes, and then click the Update Listing button when you're done.

- **Delete your listing.** To delete your ad, on the My Listings page (click Marketplace in the Applications menu, and then click the My Listings link), scroll down to the ad you want to delete and click Remove. Then, in the confirmation box that appears, turn on either the Yes radio button (if you're removing the ad because you sold the item) or the No radio button (if you're deleting the ad for some other reason), and then click Remove.

# Finding Stuff

Facebook gives you several ways to find what you're looking for in the Marketplace. From the Marketplace Home page (get there by heading to the Applications menu and clicking Marketplace), you can:

- **Browse listings by network.** Facebook assumes you want to see listings associated with your primary network, but you can see the listings for additional networks by clicking the Other tab. In the box that appears, type the name of a city or network, and then click Browse Network.

- **Browse listings by category.** There's no point in seeing ads for homes for sale if you need a job. To see all the job listings associated with a network, click the Jobs link; to see all the free-to-good-home listings, click the Free Stuff link; and so on.

- **Search for an item within a category.** To search a category, in the Search field, type the item you're looking for (such as "kitten" or "duplex"), and then choose a category (such as For Sale or Housing) from the drop-down menu. Depending on the category you choose, you see additional subcategories, along with boxes you can use to narrow your search by entering minimum and maximum prices and condition.

Marketplace Home | My Listings (2) | My Friends' Listings | Add a new listing

### ▦ Rio Grande Valley, TX Marketplace - **Item Wanted**

**Rio Grande Valley, TX**   **Other...**

Search: 🔍 _____   Item Wanted ▼   Search

Price: min   max   Condition: any ▼

Books (7)  Furniture  Tickets (1)  Electronics (8)  Cars (4)  Other (4)

Monday, October 22, 2007                                    Spons

- **See ads your friends have placed.** On the Marketplace Home page, click the My Friends' Listings link.

> **Note** Facebook encourages its members to be their brothers' keepers. If you run across an ad that rubs you the wrong way—whether it's for Nazi memorabilia or is just in the wrong category—click the Report link that appears next to every listing to send the Facebook team a heads-up.

# Answering an Ad

For privacy reasons, Marketplace listings rarely include direct contact info, such as a phone number. Instead, you answer an ad by sending a Facebook message. Here's how:

1. **From the Marketplace Home page (to get there, click Marketplace in the Applications menu), click the name of the listing you want to respond to.** Facebook displays the full ad, complete with pictures (if the person who placed it supplied pictures).

FREE - Free Kitten!
Free kitten to a loving home. She is about 2 month...
Listed by Amy Tegge in Free Stuff : Free Items | Report

2. **Do a quick reality check.** See how many times this ad has been viewed (the number is below the poster's name), which gives you an idea of whether the item is still available. Then click the name of the person who listed the ad; this sends you to his profile, which you can browse to get a feel for whether you want to conduct business with this person.

3. **To answer the ad, click the "Send a Message to [Name]" link.** Then fill out the Subject and Message fields and click Send.

# Hiring and Getting Hired

I n real life, people hire and fire based on info they get through the grape-vine—in other words, through their social networks: "You're looking for a programmer? My brother-in-law's the best programmer on the planet! Here's his number." Or, "They're hiring down at my gym. You should throw them a resumé."

Because Facebook's whole *raison d'être* is social networking, it should come as no surprise that the site can be a great help in job searches. This chapter shows you how to work the job pool from both angles. If you're looking for an employee or intern, you can use Facebook to recruit and vet prospects. If you're job hunting, you can research jobs and make connections with people who might help you get hired.

# Recruiting New Hires

Technically, unless you sign up for one of Facebook's official ad programs such as *sponsored groups* (page 200), advertising to fill an open position (or advertising for anything else) is strictly forbidden according to the site's terms of use (page 4): "You understand that except for advertising programs offered by us on the Site...the Service and the Site are available for your personal, non-commercial use only."

Whether or not you choose to pay to advertise your openings on the site, perhaps the most useful feature of Facebook is how you can put your social network to work identifying job openings and candidates for you.

## Paid Advertising

If your company has the budget for it, you might want to pay for advertising spots such as *sponsored groups* dedicated to hiring recruits. These full-blown marketing campaigns—which *start* at somewhere around six figures—let employers describe their company, what kind of employees they're looking for, what internships and job opportunities they offer, and other pertinent details. Downloadable brochures, audio and video clips, links to press releases, and polls help employers get the word out. The sponsored group's discussion board and wall (page 67) let prospects ask questions and send messages directly to the company's HR staff.

## Using Regular Facebook Groups

If your company doesn't have big bucks to spend on Facebook recruiting, you have other options. One is to create a regular, garden variety group—page 110 shows you how—and use the group to describe your company and the kinds of positions you need to fill.

**The LOUNGE**

**Information**

**Group Info**

Name:          The LOUNGE
Type:          Business - Companies
Description:   The Lounge is a new Service concept, with happy colors and feel @ home atmosphere. The Menus are Fresh and Inovative and the Shisha Tobaco is designed by our own Team to meet various tastes. Many New Flavors to Experience Only @ The Lounge : )

**Contact Info**

Email:         the_lounge_prosperos@hotmail.com

Website:       Soon
Street:        43 Ankara St . Sheraton
City:          Cairo, Egypt

**Recent News**

The AMSTEL Lounge is now Available @ the Lounge with fluffy pillows, high tables, nice visuals and special AMSTEL Cocktails.

AMSTEL ZERO, Unlimited Refreshment, Zero Alcohol.

Flip flops & Shorts are allowed now

Regular groups don't have the slick look-and-feel of sponsored groups, but the price is right—they're free. But tread lightly: Facebook gets to decide what's advertising and what's not, and the penalty for breaking its terms of use can include getting kicked off the site. To be on the safe side, keep your recruitment message low-key. To create a company-related group that's effective (but that shouldn't get you kicked off Facebook):

- When you create your group, make sure you choose the Business category.
- Include a link to your company's Web site.
- Provide an email address for someone in your HR department.
- Post your job listings in the Recent News section.
- Don't use your group to advertise your products. (For that, you want to look into free Facebook *Pages*—see page 182.)

- Monitor your discussion board. You want to jump on potential recruits as quickly as possible by following up on discussion board leads.

**Note** As this book goes to press, Facebook's marketing and advertising policies are undergoing some big changes, including the introduction of advertising *Pages* that may replace business groups—or at least affect the way you can use them. See page 182 for details.

## Posting a Marketplace Ad

One of the first things a job hunter will likely check is the Facebook Marketplace. Posting a "help wanted" add in the Marketplace is quick and easy (see page 136).

New York, NY Marketplace - Jobs - **Restaurant/Retail**

| Rio Grande Valley, TX | New York, NY | < Drop | Change... |

Search: [ ]   Restaurant/Retail

Saturday, November 3, 2007

**$10.00/hr - Part-Time Job Available**
DessertTruck, a new mobile food vending concept, i...
Listed by Chris Chen in Jobs : Restaurant/Retail | Report

Wednesday, October 31, 2007

**HELP WANTED!!!!**
Upscale golf and country club is looking for food ...
Listed by J. Luis Nunez in Jobs : Restaurant/Retail | Report

Tuesday, October 30, 2007

**New restaurant in search of several positions**
Brand new NYC restaurant, called GUSTO ORGANICS, t...
Listed by Gabriel Scott-Dicker in Jobs : Restaurant/Retail | Report

Make sure you categorize your posting appropriately; otherwise, it'll be hard to find. So, when you're filling out the Jobs form (see page 134), spend some time figuring out which category in the Job Type drop-down list best matches the position you're trying to fill.

Marketplace > Listing > Jobs

**Position:**
(required)

**Job Type:**
(required) ---

**Description:**
(required)

**Hours:** ● Full-Time ○ Part-Time

**Other Stuff:** ☐ Internship ☐ Seasonal Job ☐ Non-Profit

**Compensation:** Salary ▾ starting at $ [     ] USD change currency

**Profile:** ☑ Add this listing to my profile

**List Where:** Insert this listing in the following networks:
☑ Rio Grande Valley, TX (10,722)

**Privacy:** ☑ Let people outside of the selected networks above view this listing

**Photo(s):** [          ] Browse...

By creating a listing, you are agreeing to the Marketplace Guidelines

Create Listing    Cancel

# Searching for Prospects

Not everyone tells the truth on Facebook, but people looking for jobs generally do. These folks often pack their profiles with professional details such as their current job title, the company they work for, and even their skills and interests—all of which are easy to search for in Facebook. (See page 151 for more on using your profile as a resumé.)

To search for prospective hires:

1. **On the left side of any Facebook page, click the down arrow next to Search and then, on the menu that appears, click Advanced Search.**

2. **On the page that appears, scroll down to the Personal Info section and, in the Activities or Interests text field (or both), type the skills you're looking for.** When you finish, click Advanced Search at the bottom of the page.

> **Tip** Other fields you may want to fill in include School Status, Concentration (that is, major), Company, and Position. It's best to do a separate search for each of these criteria—you probably won't find anyone who matches *all* the things you're searching for.

| Land Phone | | |
|---|---|---|
| | | |

| Personal Info: | Activities | TV Shows |
|---|---|---|
| | gaming | |
| | Interests | Movies |
| | computers | |
| | Music | Books |
| | | |

| Education Info: | School Status | Concentration |
|---|---|---|
| | Alumnus/Alumna ▼ | Computer Information Systems |
| | Class Year | HS Year |
| | ▼ | ▼ |

| Work Info: | Company | Position |
|---|---|---|
| | | programmer |

Advanced Search   Clear

3. **Comb through your search results, check out the most promising people's profiles, and contact the folks you're interested in.**

# Announcing an Opening to Your Friends

Facebook's real strength is the way it connects you to other people through friends and acquaintances you have in common. And you don't even need to spend an evening at a cocktail party to get in touch with them. Here's how to get the most out of an offhand mention that you're looking to hire:

1. **Make sure your privacy settings are letting the buzz through.** See page 231 for guidance on adjusting your news feed and mini-feed privacy settings. At the very least, turn on the "Write a Wall Post" and "Post on a Discussion Board" checkboxes.

**News Feed and Mini-Feed Privacy**
Back to Privacy Overview without saving changes.

Facebook will only publish stories about you on your Mini-Feed and in the News Feeds of your friends.

Stories are published when you edit your profile information, join a new network, or update your Status. Also publish stories when you...

- ☐ Remove Profile Info
- ☑ Write a Wall Post
- ☐ Comment on a Note
- ☐ Comment on a Photo
- ☐ Comment on a Video
- ☐ Comment on a Posted Item
- ☑ Post on a Discussion Board
- ☐ Add a Friend

2. **Mention your job opening on your wall, or on one of your friends' walls.** Be specific (and succinct—under 20 words is best) about the type of candidate you're looking for. Not only does your post stay on the wall for prospective recruits to find, but your friends all see your brief description in their news feeds.

3. **If you (or someone else at your company) created a Marketplace listing, share it.** Clicking the Share icon at the bottom of a Marketplace listing lets you post the official job description on your profile or email it directly to people you think might be interested.

This kind of fishing expedition is so unobtrusive it's guaranteed not to cause hard feelings. And if one of your friends is interested in the job—or knows someone who is—they know how to get in touch with you.

**Note** You can also try posting a quickie job announcement on an appropriate business group's discussion board. (See page 155 for more info.)

# Vetting Prospects

Running online background checks on potential candidates—especially for high-tech and computer-related jobs—is pretty common these days: It's cheap, quick, and eye-opening in ways that formal interviews and resumés aren't.

It takes all of two seconds to conduct a Facebook background check on a candidate: Just head to the Search box in the upper-left part of any Facebook page, type in the person's name, and hit Return.

**Note** For the complete scoop on searching, check out page 36.

The profile that appears may or may not contain the truth, the whole truth, and nothing but the truth about the person—but it probably tells you *something* useful. In addition to obvious red flags (such as pictures of the candidate passed out naked), check for mutual friends who may be able to give you candid feedback about the prospect. (If you have friends in common, a Mutual Friends section appears below the person's profile picture.)

**Tip** Clicking the Share button at the bottom of a profile lets you send the person's profile information to other members of your hiring team.

**Tip** If you're having trouble finding the candidate on Facebook but have reason to believe he's a member, check with your company's HR department to see if you have anyone on staff who happens to share the candidate's alma mater or former employer. If so, that someone should be able to access the prospect's profile, since he's eligible to join the prospect's Facebook networks.

# Looking for a Job

Facebook is a terrific tool for anyone searching for a gig. Not only can you use your profile as a combination multimedia resumé/portfolio, but you can also use Facebook for professional networking *and* for tapping into your friends' expertise and contacts. Read on to learn how.

**Note** A quick search of Facebook's Application Directory (for "jobs" and "employment") yields dozens of Facebook applications designed to help you land gainful employment. Chapter 12 shows you how to find and install applications.

# Turning Your Profile into a Resumé

If you're serious about making Facebook part of your job hunt, the first thing to do is assume that every potential hiring manager can see your entire profile, and build your profile accordingly. You don't want your dream job to slip through your fingers because of a stupid comment, a way-too-candid photo, or membership in a group that celebrates illegal activities. Maybe you mean it all as a joke, but that doesn't matter: If you have an unprofessional profile, a hiring manager will take one look at it and see, at the very least, poor judgment and a total lack of understanding of how the Web works.

 **Note** Chapter 13 shows you several ways to hide profile information, but it also explains why you can't trust that your profile information will stay hidden.

Here are some ways to spiff up your profile to help you land a job:

- **Fill out the Education and Work sections of your profile completely.** Use all the industry buzzwords you can in the Description field (see page 13).

- **Describe your job-related skills in the Activities and Interests fields of the Personal section of your profile.** Because these fields are easy for potential employers to search, pack them with descriptions of your technical abilities and your interpersonal skills.

- **Do work-related stuff on Facebook.** Post regular, impressive notes that relate to your current job or job-related interests; start work-related interest groups; hold work-related events; upload samples of your work such as reports, slideshows, video or audio clips, photos, or applications you've written; befriend as many industry movers-and-shakers as you can.

- **Present yourself professionally.** Keep the silly astrology and zombie applications (see Chapter 12) to a minimum, choose your friends carefully, and don't write anything on anybody's wall that you wouldn't feel comfortable writing on a whiteboard at work.

- **Edit your feed preferences so you know when your friends add friends (page 173).** This will alert you to potential contacts. Surf to the newly added friend's profile, read up on her, and—if appropriate—approach her as a "friend of a friend." (As in, send her a message [page 60]; *don't* poke her! Poking isn't very professional—see page 66.)

- **Don't assume that potential employers *won't* be able to access your networks or your profile.** In all probability, they can and will (see page 149).

# Using the Marketplace

Facebook hopes its Marketplace will become the go-to place for jobs (and sofas, and roommates, and all the other transactions that make up day-to-day life). Marketplace is a relatively new application, and it *is* ramping up fast. But, as this book goes to press, it's a little skimpy on bona fide job listings. (In other words, *www.monster.com* and *www.craigslist.org* probably aren't feeling particularly threatened just yet.) Still, it's worth spending some time checking out the Marketplace. At the very least:

- **Browse Marketplace Jobs.** It takes only a few seconds to see whether the Marketplace lists any job openings in your area and your field. To scope things out, in the Applications menu, click Marketplace. On the Marketplace page that appears, click the Jobs link.

On the Jobs page that appears, you see numbers after some categories—these represent how many job listings are in each category. No number, no listings. If there's a number after a category you're interested in, click the category's name to see the listings.

- **Search Marketplace Jobs.** If you know precisely what you're after— a specific job title, location, or company, for example—you can get quicker results by searching Marketplace than by browsing. To search Marketplace jobs, head to the top of the Jobs page and click the tab for the network you want to search. (If you don't see a tab for the network, click the Change tab to select a different network.) Type the job you're looking for in the Search field, and then choose a job category (such as Accounting/Finance) from the drop-down list next to the search field. Finally, click Search to see the listings that match your criteria.

---

Marketplace Home | My Listings (2) | My Friends' Listings | Add a new listing     Help

🖼 **Los Angeles, CA Marketplace - Jobs - Writing/Editing**

| Los Angeles, CA | Other... |

Search: 🔍 editor     | Writing/Editing ▾ | Search

In addition to the results below, 225 results matched your query on all of Facebook. See them.

Sunday, October 7, 2007

**Editor for 300 film project at LMU**
Looking for an editor for my 300 film.
Listed by Matt Nagorner in Jobs : Writing/Editing | Report

Wednesday, August 29, 2007

**Web editor**
Yo dudes if you're interested in being the L....
Listed by Celeste Tabora in Jobs : Writing/Editing | Report

Wednesday, July 11, 2007

**Part Time Content Editor**
Internet Brands is a leading operator of media and...
Listed by Internet Brands in Jobs : Writing/Editing | Report

Sponsored Listings

**Italian speaking editor for a ...**
We are looking for an italian speak...

**Part Time Content Editor**
Internet Brands is a leading operat...

**$100 - Tech Deal ...**
Savvy web user will publish tech de...

- **Post a "Looking for Work" ad.** While it's probably not the quickest route to a new gig, creating a "Here are my qualifications and what I'm looking for" listing in Marketplace couldn't hurt—and it's easy to do: In the Applications menu, click Marketplace; then, on the right side of the Marketplace Home page that appears, click the "List what you want" button. Up pops the Marketplace Wanted page. Select the "Looking for Work" category and fill out the form that appears to create your listing.

**Tip** Include as many job-specific keywords as you can in the Objective/Skills field to help potential employers find you (especially if your skills are unique). And make sure to leave all the form's checkboxes turned on so your listing reaches as many people as possible.

Marketplace > Wanted > **Looking for Work**

| | |
|---|---|
| **Position:** (required) | |
| **Job Type:** (required) | --- |
| **Objective/Skills:** (required) | |
| **Profile:** | ☑ Add this listing to my profile |
| **List Where:** | Insert this listing in the following networks: ☑ Rio Grande Valley, TX (10,687) |
| **Privacy:** | ☑ Let people outside of the selected networks above view this listing |
| **Photo(s):** | Browse... |

By creating a listing, you are agreeing to the Marketplace Guidelines

Create Listing | Cancel

# Networking

Networking—finding out who knows who and letting all of 'em know what you have to offer—is what Facebook is all about. Here are a few ways you can put your networking skills to good use in your job search:

- **Join industry-related groups and attend industry-related events.** Doing so shows the world you're truly interested in your line of work. It also gives you the opportunity to network in person and stay current on what's happening in your field. If you don't see a group or event that fits the bill, create one.

**Tip** To see the groups your friends are members of, from the Applications menu, choose Groups. Then browse the "Recently joined by your friends" list that appears. To see the events your friends are attending, from the Applications menu, choose Events, then Friends' Events.

- **Use Advanced Search to track down old co-workers and current contacts.** It's easy to start a conversation when you can point to specific things in someone's profile. ("Small world, eh, Fred? *I* went back and picked up my master's degree after I left Acme Widgets, too!") To use Advanced Search, click the down arrow next to Search, and then click Advanced Search in the drop-down menu.

- **Let your friends know you're looking.** Instead of just sending private messages, consider tweaking your feed preferences and then writing a brief note on your wall about the kind of job you want (see page 68).

# 10

# Collaborating on Projects via Facebook

E xpensive groupware, workflow management tools, and other collaboration programs have been around for quite a while. With its open-door policy and privacy concerns (see Chapter 13), Facebook is certainly no replacement for a dedicated, bulletproof collaboration program like Lotus Domino or Novell Groupwise. But you might find that some of Facebook's tools are a handy—and free—way to help your team get work done quickly. This chapter gives Facebook's messaging and subscription tools (which Chapters 4 through 7 introduced you to) a decidedly business spin. You'll see how to use them to keep team members, co-workers, and clients in the loop—and projects on track.

# Keeping in Touch

The same Facebook features that let you and your friends "talk" online—*messaging* (page 60), *events* (page 119), *groups* (page 103), and *notes* (page 90)—can help you keep up-to-date with co-workers, clients, and customers.

> **Note** A recent study reported by *CNET.com* found that nearly half of all employers block access to social networking sites such as Facebook. The top two reasons? Loss of productivity and security concerns such as those explained in Chapter 13. If your employer won't let you use Facebook at work, you can probably skip this chapter—unless you want to collaborate on non-work projects using Facebook.

The features themselves work the same way whether you're interacting with your old college roommate or your boss. But there are a few things you need to keep in mind when you're using these features for work:

- **Professionalism.** Email did more to lower professional communication standards than casual Friday ever did. And now that everyone's finally adjusted to emoticons, here comes Facebook, a site so hip, hot, and happening—and so easy to use—that it doesn't just encourage you to be informal; it practically *orders* you. The thing is, you never know who might view your Facebook exploits, even if you're scrupulous about privacy (see Chapter 13). So, instead of thinking of Facebook as an employee lunchroom, think of it as a meeting that the big brass might drop in on at any time. Keep personal information, off-color jokes, and "just for fun" applications (page 207) to a bare minimum.

- **Privacy.** If you're using Facebook for business, you'll want to scale back on the notifications Facebook sends out about your activities. That way your boss won't get barraged with details of, say, your love life. In particular, you want to adjust your poke, message, friend request, news feed, and mini-feed privacy settings (see pages 230 and 101, respectively). You may even want to pare down your profile to create a *limited profile* (page 226) suitable for business contacts.

- **Security.** Be careful not to discuss anything mission-critical on Facebook, and don't post confidential company documents of any kind. And because you can't be sure that information you give the site won't get out, you may even want to keep mum about things like your work phone number and travel itinerary.

# Sending Messages

Whether you're an employee working in a cubicle farm or a freelancer working from home, you've probably already got an email program. So, why use Facebook to send and receive messages? Two reasons:

1. **It's super easy.** If your co-workers and clients are on Facebook, sending them message takes only one click—whether you want to invite them to an impromptu meeting, comment on a document or Web site one of them posted, or share a video clip. (Thank the Message All Members, "Send [somebody] a Message", Share, and other click-to-contact links scattered around the site.)

> **Note** If some of your co-workers and clients aren't on Facebook, check out page 41 for an easy way to invite them to join.

2. **It helps you organize your correspondence.** If your team uses Facebook to collaborate on a project, Facebook's messaging feature helps you keep project-specific correspondence separate from your other work-related email.

# Setting up Meetings

Intranets (private Web sites that only company employees can access) are great for lining up in-house meetings, but Facebook *events* are a handy way to organize get-togethers that involve a mix of co-workers and "civilians" such as clients, potential clients, suppliers, and former employees.

> **Note** For the full scoop on Facebook events, flip to page 119.

The thing you want to pay attention to when organizing an event is the level of access that you grant other people (see page 120). So after you choose Events from the Applications menu and then click "Create an Event" to display the "Create an Event: Step 1: Event Info" page, do the following:

Show the guest list.

☑ Enable the wall.

☑ Enable photos.

   ⦿ Allow all members to upload photos.

   ◯ Only allow admins to upload photos.

☑ Enable videos.

   ⦿ Allow all members to upload videos.

   ◯ Only allow admins to upload videos.

☑ Enable posted items.

   ⦿ Allow all members to post items.

   ◯ Only allow admins to post items.

**Access:**    ◯ This event is open.

People can add themselves to the guest list and invite others to the event. Anyone can see the event information, the guest list, the wall, videos of the event, and photos of the event.

◯ This event is closed.

Only people you invite will be on the guest list. People can request invitations. Anyone can see the event time and description, but only those invited can see the location, the guest list, the wall, videos of the event, and photos of the event.

⦿ This event is secret.

The event will not appear in search results. Only people you invite can see the event information, the guest list, the wall, videos of the event, and photos of the event.

- **Restrict your event to your company's network.** Choose the correct network from the Network drop-down list (hint: it's probably *not* the Global network).

- **Turn on the "This event is secret" radio button**. Doing so keeps details of your event out of non-attendees' searches and news feeds.

- **Decide how much access to grant attendees.** If you expect meeting materials to flow just one way—for example, if you plan to post documents or multimedia files for attendees to review, but don't see a need for them to post stuff—turn off the Enable checkboxes. (Doing so helps prevent confusion, as well as the more serious threat of breached confidentiality in cases where, for example, you want to make sure nobody uploads confidential company documents.) If you don't want anyone to know who's attending the meeting—say it's a sales meeting and you don't want your attendees to get together without you before you've had a chance to give your official pitch—turn off the "Show the guest list" checkbox.

# Exchanging Ideas

Facebook *groups* (page 103) are terrific for:

- **User groups and other customer-oriented information exchanges.** You get to combine your company logo with Facebook's groovy collaboration features (such as a moderated discussion board, the ability to exchange files, and one-click messaging to all group members) to build or maintain interest in your company and products—for free!

> **Note** Technically, Facebook is for non-commercial use only—but gobs of people are using groups for marketing, and Facebook's SWAT team doesn't seem to mind (at least, not yet). See Chapter 11 for more on using Facebook for commercial purposes.

- **Team discussions.** If your company doesn't have an intranet and is relying instead on email for team discussions, you're going to love Facebook groups. Using groups is a lot easier than dealing with mile-long "me too" replies and CC lists—*and* groups give people a single place to go for updates and file exchanges. Just be sure you restrict your group to your company's network and make your group secret (see page 111). This keeps group details out of the hands of riffraff (meaning anybody who's not a confirmed team member).

Chapter 6 has all the details about setting up and using groups.

## Creating and Subscribing to Notes

Facebook *notes* (page 90) are basically blog entries people can subscribe to. You *could* use plain old email to send your team multimedia documents like project milestones, ongoing customer service requests, or meeting minutes. But using Facebook notes instead gives team members the best of both worlds: Web feeds (page 84) that alert them every time you post a new document, and a single, easily-accessible archive of everything you've posted.

To use notes:

- **Make sure all your team members are on your Friend List.** See page 52.

- **Adjust your notes settings.** On the "Privacy Settings for Notes" page (page 96), restrict access to "Only my friends", and then zip to the Syndication section and make sure the "Anyone who can see my notes can subscribe to my notes" radio button is turned on. If it's not, turn it on.

- **Have your team members subscribe to your notes.** Have each of them go to any of your notes and scroll to the "Subscribe to these Notes" section on the right side of the page, and then click the "[Your Name]'s Notes" link. On the page that appears, each person needs to click "Subscribe to this feed". (See page 84 for more on subscribing to feeds.)

# Exchanging Files

It doesn't matter whether you're talking team meetings, sales conferences, or product launches: All business interactions generate documents. Brochures, diagrams, attendee lists, action items, reports, recommendations, flow charts—the list goes on and on. Fortunately, one of the things Facebook excels at is letting you exchange documents painlessly and privately.

> **Note** Privacy, of course, is relative. No free site will ever guard your data as carefully as you would. See Chapter 13 for the whole scoop on Facebook privacy. The bottom line: Don't use Facebook to send confidential info.

Facebook's built-in Photos application lets you upload and share image files with your co-workers. And the built-in Posted Items application lets you share just about anything else, from audio and video clips to files and documents stored on the Web. Read on to learn how, or see page 206 to learn about applications.

# Sharing Pictures

You can use Facebook's Photos application to upload and share picture files. The files you upload have to be in one of these three Internet-friendly formats: .jpg; .png (with some restrictions—see page 165); and .gif (but *not* animated .gifs).

**Tip** If you're not sure what format a picture file is in, here's how to find out: Locate the file on your computer and right-click it (Ctrl-click on a Mac); then select Properties (Get Info) from the pop-up menu that appears. The info box you see lists the file's format.

On Facebook, you organize your picture files by grouping them into *albums*. You can limit access to each album so that only certain team members can see it, and you can even *tag* individual pictures. (*Tagging* is a way of associating one or more team members with the picture, which is useful for establishing and tracking accountability. For example, you can tag a picture of a features list so that each list item is associated with the person responsible for developing it.)

**Note** Albums aren't the only way to share pictures. In addition to your profile picture (page 15), Facebook lets you add pictures to groups, events, and notes. But using the Photos application's albums is your best bet when you want to keep project- or team-related photos, drawings, sketches, or screenshots in one place.

# Creating and Filling a Picture Album

Before you can upload and share a group of picture files, you need to create an album. Here's how to do both:

1. **From the Applications menu, choose Photos.**

Because Photos is an application, you can delete it (see page 213). If you deleted it by accident, turn to page 208 to learn how to find and reinstall it.

2. **On the Photos page that appears, click the "Create a Photo Album" button.**

My Photos | Photos of You | Photo Printshop                                     Help

📷 **Photos**                                                   ( + **Create a Photo Album** )

**Recent Photo Albums**  **Recently Tagged Friends**

Your friends have not created any photo albums yet.

You can upload your own or find more friends.

3. **Describe your photo album, and then click "Create Album".** Whatever you type in for the Name, Location, and Description fields will be visible to everyone who can see your album, so keep it clean. From the "Visible to" drop-down list, choose "Only my friends" to restrict album access to your team members.

📷 **Add New Photos**

**Create Album**  **Mobile Photos**

Name:    Acme Photography--Little Miss RGV account

Location:    Brownsville, Texas

Description:    These are all possible shots for the LMRGV 2008 calendar. Walt, we need you and the rest of the board to give us the thumbs-up on half-size or full-size based on these.

Visible to:    Only my friends

Create Album    Cancel

4. **Decide whether you need to upload lots of pictures at once.** On the Upload Photos page that appears, Facebook gives you two options:

— Let Facebook install a little software module called an *ActiveX component* (sometimes referred to as an ActiveX *control*) on your computer that you can use to upload lots of .jpg or .gif files—but not .png files—all at once (but which, like all ActiveX components, represents a slight security risk). You can think of an ActiveX component as a special kind of plug-in that works inside Microsoft programs such as Internet Explorer.

The ActiveX component really is slick. Unless you're hyper security-conscious or plan to only ever upload two or three picture files to Facebook, install it! It lets you preview each photo, turn on checkboxes to select pictures, and even rotate individual pictures before uploading them.

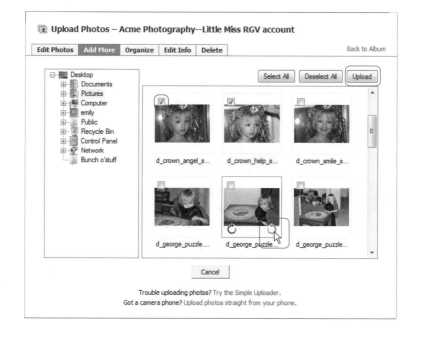

> **Note** Attention Mac fans: The batch uploading tool you get is delivered via a Java add-in rather than ActiveX; the behind-the-scenes differences are details only a programmer would want to know. The good news for you: Java provides all the same tricks as ActiveX but with an even more minuscule security risk.

— Go with a bare bones, one-at-a-time uploading feature that doesn't require you to download a potentially dangerous mini-program and lets you upload .png files.

To install the ActiveX component, click either the Download button you see on the pop-up window or (if you've got pop-ups turned off in your browser) the "click here to install the ActiveX control" bar at the top of your browser. To install the other, slower uploading feature, click the "Try the Simple Uploader" link.

5. **Tell Facebook which picture files you want to upload.** The Upload Photos page you see depends on the uploading feature you chose in step 4. If you went with the ActiveX photo upload tool, you can click to browse your computer for picture files and select a bunch of them all at once. If you chose the Simple Uploader, the page lets you browse your computer and select files one at a time. After you choose the files you want to upload, click either the Upload or Upload Photos button.

**Note** The picture files you choose need to weigh in at less than 5 megabytes each. See the Tip on page 163 with details about checking a photo's file format; the info box that appears also shows you file size.

**Note** The ActiveX photo upload tool's page requires you to turn on an "I certify that I have the right to distribute these photos" checkbox before you can post your photos. But even though you don't have to turn on any special checkboxes on the Simple Uploader's Upload Photos page, by uploading picture files using either page, you're guaranteeing that the files you're uploading are yours to share.

## Editing Your Album

After you create an album, you can change practically anything about it. From the Edit Album page (which you get to by heading to the Photos section of your profile, clicking the name of your album, and then clicking the "Edit Photos" link), you can:

- **Add more pictures.** Click Add More Photos and then, on the Upload Photos page that appears, follow the same steps you used to upload your first batch of picture files (page 165).

- **Delete pictures.** Scroll to the picture you want to delete and turn on the "Delete this photo" checkbox below it. (To delete multiple pictures, turn on each picture's checkbox.) Then head to the bottom of the page and click the Save Changes button.

**Note** To delete a whole album, click the Delete Album link.

- **Reorder your pictures.** Click Organize Photos and, on the page that appears, either drag the pictures into the order you want them, or click the Reverse Order button (which moves pictures A, B, and C so C shows up first, then B, then A). When you finish, click the Save Changes button.

- **Add captions to pictures.** Head to a picture and type your caption text in the Caption field. Don't forget to click Save Changes when you're done.

**Note** Your caption text pops up when people mouse over a picture in your album.

We're going to replace the background on most of these, but definitely this one. Cropping's also a possibilty.

- **Choose a picture to use as the album's "cover."** Facebook assumes you want the first picture you uploaded to be your album's cover, but you can tell it differently. To pick your own cover, scroll to the picture you want to appear as a thumbnail (a tiny image) on your profile page (and wherever else Facebook displays your album, such as in your mini-feed when you update your album, or in an email message you've attached your album to). Click the "This is the album cover" radio button next to the photo, and then head to the bottom of the page and click Save Changes.

- **Change the name or description of your album.** Click the Edit Info tab, make your changes, and then click Save Changes.

**Tip** Clicking the Edit Info tab displays a link you can use to share your album with people who aren't Facebook members. Simply copy and paste the link into an email.

# Viewing Your Album

After you create an album, Facebook displays a thumbnail of the album's cover (page 168) on the Photos section of your profile. When someone clicks on the album's name, Facebook displays album info along with links to each picture in the album.

**Note** Everyone who can see your full profile can see your photos, but folks who can see your photos can't necessarily see your profile. That's because Facebook lets you set access to your profile and to your albums separately—see page 225.

# Restricting Access to Your Albums

Facebook gives you a couple different ways to control who can see your albums:

- **Specify who can see you albums.** You did this when you created your album, but you can change this setting at any time: From the Edit Album page (page 167), click Edit Album Info, and then choose one of the following from the "Visible to" drop-down list:

  — Everyone

  — All my networks and all my friends

  — Some of my networks and all my friends

  — Only my friends

- **If you create** *limited profiles* **(page 226) for certain people on your team, you can hide one or more albums from them.** For example, say you set up a limited profile for team members who are contract workers instead of company employees. You can put employee-only pictures into an album and hide that album from anyone viewing your limited profile. To do so: At the top right of any Facebook page, click the "privacy" link. Then scroll down to the Limited Profile section of the page that appears and click Edit Settings. On the Limited Profile

Settings page, scroll down to the Photo Albums section, turn off the checkbox next to the album (or albums) you want to hide, and then click Save.

## Tagging (Labeling) Your Pictures

*Tagging* is a nifty way to add a virtual label to your images. You can use tags to identify individuals in group pictures, but tagging is also a handy way to indicate who's responsible for creating or working on something shown in a picture. For example, tagging each section of a flow chart or schematic with a co-worker's name lets everyone know who's responsible for what, quickly and easily.

Every time someone looks at your photo album (page 169), he sees a list of all the people tagged in that album. Clicking the "photos" link next to a name lets you see all the pictures in all the albums that are associated with that person.

These are all possible shots for the LMRGV 2008 calendar. W
the rest of the board to give us the thumbs-up on half-size o
these.

Location: Brownsville, Texas

In this album: Emily Moore (photos)

Then, when he mouses over the tagged portion of a picture, up pops the tagee's name.

To tag a picture:

1. **From the Edit Album page (page 167), mouse over the picture you're interested in.** Your cursor turns into crosshairs.

2. **When you're right over the spot you want to tag, click.** Facebook draws a white square on the picture and pops up a box you can use to associate that section of the picture with yourself or anyone on your Friend List.

> **Note** In addition to tagging a picture from the Edit Album page, you can also tag (as well as edit, rotate, and add a caption to) a picture from an individual picture's page. To do so: From the Applications menu, choose Photos, and then click the My Photos link. Scroll down and click the picture you want to tag, and then click it again. When you scroll to the bottom of the picture's page, you see a Tag This Photo link. Click it, and then follow step 2 above.

# Posting Items on Your Profile

If you can find a link to something on the Web, you can add it to your Facebook profile. Think company documents from your corporate site, video clips from your marketing department, or relevant research you've collected from all over the Web that you want your team to see. The items you post appear in the Posted Items and Mini-Feed sections of your profile.

Unless you've blocked their access (see page 236), team members can add their comments after they've checked out each item, and they can share them with others (even non-Facebook members) quickly and easily by clicking the Share button that appears alongside each posted item.

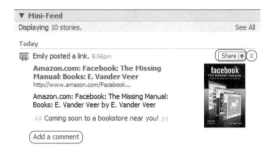

Best of all, multimedia links appear complete with controls so the people browsing your posted items can listen to music, watch a video clip, or check out other content you've posted—all without leaving your Posted Items page.

To post something:

1. **From the Applications menu, choose Posted Items.** You may have to click (or hover over) "more" to see the Posted Items link.

2. **Tell Facebook where to find the item you want to post.** On the Posted Items page that appears, head to the "Post a link" field, type or copy and paste the URL (Web address) of the item you want to post, and then click the Post button.

3. **On the "Post to My Profile" page that appears, click in the Comment field and type a note explaining why you want your team to see this item.** From the URL you specify, Facebook automatically pulls in the title of the item, a description, and any pictures the Web page contains. The title and description are usually pretty useful, but if you don't like one or both, simply click either one and start typing to write your own. Then flip through the thumbnail pictures Facebook copied from the site you linked to and either choose an image you want to appear next to your posted link or turn on the No Picture checkbox.

**Post to My Profile**

Comment:

Title

Choose a Thumbnail

◀ ▶ 1 of 18

**Amazon.com: Facebook: The Missing Manual: Books: E. Vander Veer**

Amazon.com: Facebook: The Missing Manual: Books: E. Vander Veer by E. Vander Veer http://www.amazon.com/Facebook-Miss...

Description

☐ No Picture

Post    Cancel

4. **Click Post.** The item appears on the Posted Items section of your profile. In addition, depending on your privacy settings (see pages 95 and 231), news of your newly posted item may also appear in your minifeed and in your friends' news feeds.

> **Note** To delete an item you've posted, head to your Posted Items page (from the Applications menu, choose Posted Items, and then click the My Posted Items link) and click the X next to the item's Share button.

# Keeping Up-to-date with Feeds

One of the best arguments for using Facebook on the job is *notifications* (page 81). When one of your team members updates a report, you get a notification. When another one weighs in on a discussion, you get a notification. And so on. Notifications make your life easier by automating one of the hardest things about keeping projects on track: keeping team members apprised of each others' actions and of project milestones. And you can customize these automated messages to an amazing degree. Here's how to make sure you're notified of just the important stuff:

> **Note** Facebook doesn't let you completely control the notification process. Stuff you're not interested in is bound to get through occasionally.

1. **Decide which team member activities you want Facebook to share with the group (for example, "Post on a Discussion Board" or "Add a Friend").** To change your settings, at the top right of any Facebook page, click the "privacy" link. Then click the "News Feed and Mini-Feed" link to display the "News Feed and Mini-Feed Privacy Settings" page. Adjust your settings (to control which of your activities your team members get notified about—see page 101), and then, to ensure consistent notifications among team members, tell your team members how to adjust their settings.

> **Note** For more on the "News Feed and Mini-Feed Privacy Settings" page, see page 231.

2. **Tell Facebook what kinds of activities you're most interested in and which team members you want to keep the closest eye on.** Facebook has the last word on which *stories* (newsy tidbits) appear on the News Feed section of your home page, but you can influence its selections. To do so: From your home page (click the "home" link at the top of any page to get to it), click the Preferences link to the right of the News Feed section heading. See page 79 for details on setting story preferences.

3. **Tell Facebook which activities involving you you want to be notified about.** Facebook can keep track of just about anything anybody does on the site that involves you. For example, you can tell Facebook to email you when a team member replies to one of your posts on a discussion board or comments on a note or photo you've posted. At the top of any Facebook page, click the "account" link, and then click the Notifications tab. (See page 83 for more about notification settings.)

> **Note** Notifications are a great way to keep current with your project if you travel a lot and have email access but can't log in to Facebook. (Facebook Mobile is another option.) For the skinny on notifications, flip to page 81; for the full scoop on Facebook Mobile, see Chapter 14.

# Advertising on Facebook

I n Facebook's early days, "advertising" meant college students looking to sell their old textbooks or find new roommates. But now that Facebook is open to the public and has several million members, things have changed. Facebook's ability to comb through millions of personal details at a practically unheard-of level of granularity ("Show me all the conservative male college students who live in Portland, have mobile phones, and enjoy watching vintage Bugs Bunny reruns") *and* tap directly into each member's circle of friends is an advertiser's dream come true.

These days, big companies with big ad budgets are placing ads on Facebook. As the site has grown, marketing strategies have changed, too, from simple network-targeted banner ads to *social ads*, which mine members' personal details and Friend Lists to hawk products. This chapter explores your options for advertising on Facebook, which range from free to affordable to don't even think about it.

# Taking Polls

A Facebook *poll* is a lot like its real-world counterpart: It's a question you can pay to display in certain Facebook members' news feeds. Because Facebook gives you detailed feedback—not just the answers people picked, but other useful information, too, such as what percentage of males took your poll—polls are a relatively inexpensive way to "feel out" a group of members, which you probably want to do if you're considering dropping a wad of cash on *social ads* (page 189) or a *sponsored group* (page 200). Think of polls as quick-and-dirty consumer surveys.

Here's an overview of how polls work:

1. **Tell Facebook what kind of people you want to answer your question.** You can target members based on gender, age, location, or personal interests. So, for example, you can tell Facebook to display your poll only in the news feeds of 25- to 34-year-olds, or only in the news feeds of people who list *The Grapes of Wrath* as one of their favorite books.

> **Note** If you want to use more than one characteristic to describe your poll's audience, check out *social ads* (page 189), which let you combine characteristics to come up with pinpointed target audiences such as all 18- to 24-year-old males who like *The Grapes of Wrath*.

2. **Decide what question you want to ask.** It's a good idea to keep your question short and sweet—people are more likely to read and respond to a one-sentence poll than a big ol' paragraph—and you're limited to text only: no graphics allowed.

3. **Include up to five possible answers.** Answers have to be in the form of one-choice-only clickable radio buttons; you can't throw in true/false or write-in options.

4. **Pay for your poll.** The amount you have to pony up varies based on how many responses you want, as well as how quickly you want complete poll results. Polls start at $26.

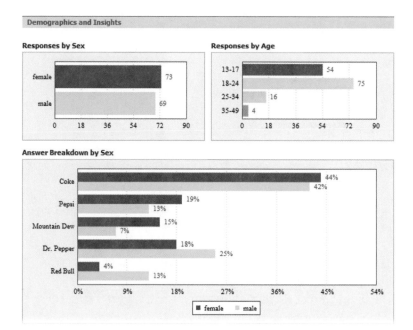

5. **Check out the results.** Facebook returns poll results in real time, so you get instant gratification as you watch the results stream in. Polls stay up for 24 hours max, but yours might close sooner depending on the number of results you paid for (see page 181). Happily, Facebook displays results in an easy-to-read visual format rather than just dumping raw data on you.

## Setting Up a Poll

If you've got your credit card handy, you're halfway to creating a Facebook poll; they're that easy to set up. Here's what you do:

1. **Scroll to the bottom of any Facebook screen and click the Businesses link.** Then, on the right side of the Business Solutions page that appears, click the Facebook Polls link.

2. **On the Polls tab, click the "Create a Facebook Poll" button.**

3. **In the form that appears, type in your poll.** Start with your question, and then type between two and five possible answers. (As soon as you start typing in the Answers field, Facebook displays another Answers field.) Then, from *one* of the "Set your Audience" drop-down lists, choose which Facebook members you want to see your poll: only males (Sex), only business majors or people into hip-hop (Interests), only people who live in Seattle (Location), and so forth. (You only get to pick one criterion; as soon as you choose one, Facebook grays out the other three drop-down lists.) When you finish, click Continue.

---

**Create a New Poll**

Ask your Question

> How many dogs are too many?

**Answers** (Enter up to 5 choices)

- 1
- 3
- 15
- No such thing as too many dogs!
- 

**Set your Audience**
(Optional: Choose a target audience for better, faster results)

| Interests | ▼ | or | Location | ▼ | or | Age | ▼ | or | Sex | ▼ |

Location
By College
By Location

Continue »

4. **In the Polls form that appears, double-check your poll to make sure you haven't misspelled anything; then pay up.** If you spot a goof in your question, answers, or the audience you selected, click the Edit Poll Details button to fix it. If you want to keep your answer choices in the order you entered them (instead of letting Facebook put them in any order it feels like), turn on the "Do not randomize my answer order" checkbox. Then set the Pricing and Max Responses options you want (the higher the Pricing option you choose, the quicker you get complete results).

**Poll Preview**

How many dogs are too many? Sponsored Poll

- 1
- 3
- 15
- No such thing as too many dogs!

☐ Do not randomize my answer order

[ Edit Poll Details ]

**Cost and Runtime**

| | |
|---|---|
| Audience: | Age 25-34 Users |
| Pricing: | $0.25 per response ▼  Est. Runtime: 24 hours |
| Max Responses: | 100 ▼ |
| Insertion Fee: | $1 |
| Max Cost: | $26 |

**Payment Information**

| | |
|---|---|
| Cardholder's Name: | |
| Credit Card Type: | Visa ▼ |

5. **Finally, head to the Payment Information section of the page, and enter your credit card info.** When you finish, click Place Order. Facebook shoots your question out to as many Facebook members as it'll take to return the number of responses you paid for.

6. **After you place your order, Facebook begins displaying poll results as they come in.** Poll results appear as soon as you click Place Order. If you surf off to do something else on Facebook, you can get back to your poll results by heading to *www.facebook.com/polls.php*.

# Facebook Pages: Profiles for Bands, Brands, and More

The unfortunately named *Pages* (could the Facebook design team have possibly come up with a more generic name?) are basically Facebook profiles for things other than people, like bands and companies. Relatively new to Facebook (they've been around only since fall 2007), Pages combine the detailed information of a personal profile with interactive features and a pretty amazing marketing scheme. And best of all, they're free.

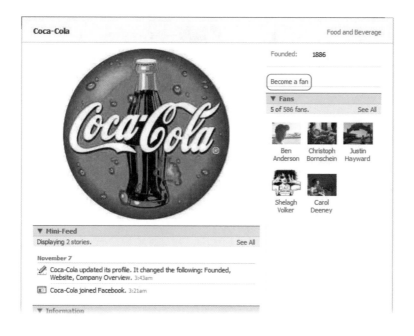

Geared toward freelancers, business owners, musicians, politicians, non-profits, and other small- to large-sized organizations, Pages:

- **Are tailored to meet your needs.** For example, say you set up a band Page (page 185 shows you how). Your Page automatically comes with the standard discussion board, wall, and photo album features. But wait, there's more: It also includes sections for posting video clips and listing upcoming events, and a built-in music player so people can check out your music.

- **Aren't subject to the 1,000-member limit Facebook places on** *groups*. Pages can have an unlimited number of fans.

- **Give your organization respectability and visibility.** You don't have to tiptoe around Facebook's advertising ban with Pages like you do with groups, because Pages were designed specifically *for* advertising. And because people searching Facebook can browse through Pages by clicking the Pages tab in their search results, they're more likely to find your Page than if it was grouped in with a million personal profiles.

- **Don't cost you anything.** If you want to shoot social ads (page 189) to all your Page's fans, you'll need to get out your credit card; but for now, creating a Page is completely free.

## How Pages Work

Word of mouth is an effective marketing scheme offline, and it works online, too. When a Facebook member surfs to a Page—by searching, browsing, or following a link he finds on another Facebook member's profile—and likes what he sees, he signs up as a *fan* of the Page (see page 187), and then all kinds of interesting things happen:

- **Facebook lists the Page on his profile.** Everyone who visits this guy's Page will now see that he's coo coo for Cocoa Puffs (or likes the band, brand, or nonprofit organization he declared himself a fan of).

- **News of the guy's new fan status appears both in his mini-feed (page 80) and in his friends' news feeds (page 78).**

- **The person or company who created the Page gets to see who's viewing it and how often via Insights (page 190). The Page's creator also gets the option of sending news blasts called *updates* (page 188) to the fan.** For a fee, the Page's creator can also send targeted *social ads* (page 189) to the fan *and* to everyone on the fan's Friend List (page 50).

# Creating a Page

Here's how to create a free Facebook Page for your business, band, or non-profit:

1. **Scroll to the bottom of any Facebook screen and click the Businesses link.** Then, on the right side of the Business Solutions page that appears, click the Facebook Pages link. On the Facebook Pages screen, click the "Create a Facebook Page" button.

2. **On the Create New Facebook Page form, choose a category and Page name.** The Local drop-down list includes business options like restaurant, park, and religious center. In other words, Local is where you indicate what kind of business you are. Turn on the "Brand or Product" radio button if you're selling products such as pharmaceuticals or food, or if you're in a business with a national reach such as travel or communications. Turning on the "Artist, Band, or Public Figure" radio button gives you freelance options such as writer, politician, and athlete. After you've picked the appropriate category and given your Page a name, click Create Page.

Frontera Jazz Quartet                                    Musician

**Your page has been created.**
To start, add information or upload a picture.

Upload a picture

Edit Page
Become a fan

▼ **Fans**
There are no fans.

▼ **Photos**                                        edit  X
No one has added any photos.
Add Photos

▼ **Video**                                         edit  X
There are no videos.
Add Videos

▼ **Mini-Feed**                              See All
Displaying 1 story.

Today
Frontera Jazz Quartet joined Facebook. 10:14pm          x

▼ **Events**                                        edit  X
There are no events.
Create Events

▼ **Information**                            edit
Add information to this page

▼ **Discography**                                   edit  X

▼ The Wall

3. **Flesh out your Page.** The first thing you want to do is click the "Upload a picture" link to replace the giant question mark with a picture
   of your band, your product, or whatever. Then click "Add information
   to this page" to build a profile similar to the personal profile you created when you joined Facebook (see page 6), by filling in Basic Info as
   well as Detailed Info. When you finish building your Page's profile, click
   the Edit Page link to see a list of all the different applications you can
   upload tidbits to (such as album info, concert dates, and music clips if
   you're in a band) and settings you can adjust (such as requiring your
   fans to be over 18).

| | Overview | Ad Campaigns | Pages |
|---|---|---|---|

**? Frontera Jazz Quartet**
Back to Pages | View Page | Delete Page

**Information**

🖼 **Profile Picture**                                                          Edit

Change the main picture that represents you on Facebook.

👤 **Basic Info**                                                                Edit

Edit members, hometown, genre, and record label.

✏ **Detailed Info**                                                             Edit

Edit website, influences, biography, general manager, current location,
booking agent, press contact, artists we also like, and band interests.

**Applications**

🎵 **Discography**                                                              Edit

Discography helps your fans track the history of your records. List your
albums as well as the tracks each one included.

📅 **Events**                                                                   Edit

4. **Publish your Page.** When you've packed your Page with as much info, photos, media clips, and other goodies as you can think of, click View Page. If it looks good, click the "publish this page" link (if not, click the "Back to Pages" link to make changes). That's it: Your Page is online.

**Note** Now that you've got a Page up, you might want to spend some money to make sure it gets noticed. Surprise! Facebook makes spending money easy. From the Applications menu, choose Page Manager (an application that Facebook installs automatically when you create a Page); then click the green "Create an ad" button. Make sure you also check out page 190 to learn how to add *social actions* to your Page.

## Becoming a Fan

Similar to wearing name-brand clothes and rooting for your favorite sports team, becoming a *fan* of a Page tells people in your social circle what you like and what's important to you.

**Note** After you create your own Page, people can become *your* fan using the steps below.

Declaring your fan status is easy. Just follow these steps:

1. **Find the Page you're interested in (type the name in the search box, and then click the Pages tab on the results page), and then click the "Become a fan" link.** This link appears on the Page itself and on the Page's listing in your search results.

2. **In the confirmation box that appears, affirm your fan status.** Turn off the "Allow [this Page] to send Updates to the Updates tab of my Facebook Inbox" checkbox if you *don't* want to hear from the Page, and then click Add. Facebook lists the Page in the "I am a Fan of…" section on your profile. News of your newfound fandom also appears in your mini-feed, and in your friends' news feeds.

**Note** This isn't your only chance to turn a Page's updates on or off. If you become a fan of a Page and later decide you don't want to get updates from it after all, head to the top of any Facebook screen and click the down arrow next to Inbox, and then select Updates from the drop-down menu. On the Updates tab that appears (which is where you see any Updates you receive), click Edit Updates Settings. Then simply turn off the checkboxes next to any Pages you don't want to hear from and click Save Changes.

**Become a fan**

When you add The Colbert Report, it will display on your profile. The Colbert Report will have no access to your individual profile information beyond your name and profile picture thumbnail. (privacy policy)

☑ Allow The Colbert Report to send Updates to the Updates tab of my Facebook Inbox.
You can edit this setting at any time.

Add    Cancel

# Social Ads (Targeted Announcements)

A *social ad* is an announcement you can broadcast to specific groups of Facebook members, such as men in their 20s, women with college degrees, or married people who work at Wal-Mart and like Beanie Babies. Every social ad consists of a graphic and a little text, and each appears either in Facebook's ad space (the lower-left part of each screen), or in people's news feeds (page 78), or both, depending on how much you pay.

**Tip** Facebook's *social actions* feature and *Beacon* program let you track people who interact with your Facebook Page or application—or with your company's Web site—and then shoot your ad out to all their friends. The result? An ad that's a little more personal and relevant—and, hopefully, more effective—than the average ad. See below for the scoop on social actions, and page 197 for more on Beacon.

Here's how social ads work:

1. **Create your ad and tell Facebook when to run it and which members to target.** You can get pretty darned specific when it comes to who sees your ad. For example, you can have Facebook show the ad only to single people aged 31 to 36 who have conservative political views and a degree in biology.

2. **Pay for the ad.** The amount you pay depends on how long you want your ad to run and how many people you want to see it.

3. **Optionally, you can tie your social ad to** *social actions*, **which are the things people do on your Facebook Page or on your company's Web site.** If you've already created a Facebook Page (page 185) or already have a Web site, you can combine your ad with the "news" headline that someone's friend just became a fan, bought your product, or otherwise interacted with your Page or site.

4. **Facebook runs your ad.** Depending on such factors as how much money you coughed up and how many other ads Facebook has in the hopper, your ad appears either in peoples' news feeds or in the space Facebook reserves for ads (the lower-left side of each screen).

5. **Get feedback that helps you assess your ad's effectiveness.** Facebook's *Insights* program generates charts that show you the kind of response your ad is getting (page 196 shows an example). If you know how to analyze them (they're pretty straightforward), these charts can help you figure out whether your ad's working or whether you need to tweak it. You get to use Insights for free when you purchase a social ad.

## Creating and Running a Social Ad

If you've got a graphic and a couple lines of copy, creating a social ad is nearly as easy as creating a Marketplace ad (page 133). Expect to spend somewhere between $5 and $50 per day, depending on who you want to reach and how long you want your ad to run.

Here's how to create and run a social ad:

1. **Scroll to the bottom of any Facebook screen and click the Advertisers link.** Then, on the Facebook Ads page that appears, click the Create Social Ad button.

2. **Tell Facebook whether you want to drive traffic to a Web site or a Facebook Page.** In the Get Started tab, click either the text field and type in the URL of your company Web site, or turn on the "Help me make a Page" radio button and create the Facebook Page (see page 182) you want people to see when they click your ad. When you're done, click Continue.

| 1. Get Started | 2. Choose Audience | 3. Create Ad | 4. Set Budget |
|---|---|---|---|

I want to reach men age 18 and older in the United States who like Jazz Band.

≈ 4,420 people

Location: United States ▼

     ⊙ Everywhere    ○ By State/Province    ○ By City

Sex: ☑ Male   ☐ Female

Age: 18 ▼ to Any ▼

Keywords: Jazz Band ✕

(interests, favorite music, movies, etc.)

Education Status: ⊙ All   ○ College Grad   ○ In College   ○ In High School

Workplaces:

Political Views: ☐ Liberal   ☐ Moderate   ☐ Conservative

Relationship Status: ☐ Single   ☐ In a Relationship   ☐ Engaged   ☐ Married

Back    Continue ▸

3. **Tell Facebook who you want to target.** As you select options on the Choose Audience tab, Facebook updates the number at the top-right of the screen to give you a rough idea of how many members are in the demographic you've chosen. (Turn on the Male checkbox, for example, and Facebook cuts the figure in half, since about half its members are female.) When you're done, click Continue.

**Tip** Clicking your browser's Back button (it probably looks like a left-facing arrow) erases all your hard work and forces you to start your ad from scratch. So, if you change your mind about one of the options you've set on a previous page while you're creating an ad, click either the tab you want to head back to (like the "2. Choose Audience" tab) or the Back button you see at the bottom of your screen.

| 1. Get Started | 2. Choose Audience | 3. Create Ad | 4. Set Budget |

**Create Your Ad**

Title: The Frontera Jazz Quartet

**The Frontera Jazz Quartet**

Body: Jazz knows no boundaries. Check it out today! Your ears will be glad you did.|

Photo: Upload a Photo ▼

Browse...

Images will be resized to fit inside a 110px by 80px box. Use 3:4 or 16:9 aspect ratio for best results.

Jazz knows no boundaries. Check it out today! Your ears will be glad you did.

Click the ad preview to test your link.

[ Back ]  [ Continue ▶ ]

---

**Tip** If you create a social ad *after* you've created a Facebook Page (page 182) or application (page 206), the Create Ad tab displays the "Add Social Actions to my ad" checkbox right below the Photo fields. Turn on the checkbox if you want to advertise directly to the friends of people who check out your Page or application. (The friends all see a personalized version of your ad that mentions someone they know and an action that person just took, which is virtually guaranteed to be more effective than the regular, generic version of your ad.)

Meredith bought tickets to Dave Matthews Band.

**Tickets on sale today!**

4. **Type in your text and upload your graphic (if you have one).** On the Create Ad tab, type in your ad's title (25 characters or less) and body text (up to 135 characters). From the Photo field, choose Upload a Photo, and then click Browse to search your computer for the picture file you want to go with your ad. After you've done all that, click Continue.

**Note** If your picture file is bigger than 4K or happens to be an animated image file, Facebook won't let you upload it. If your image is larger than 110 x 80 pixels, Facebook will upload it, but it'll shrink it to 110 x 80 pixels, so your image will be squished and people won't be able to make out any details. (See the Tip on page 163 to learn how to check an image's file format; the info box that appears also shows you file size and pixel measurements.)

5. **Decide whether you want to pay Facebook based on how many people it drives to your site or Page (*pay for clicks*), or based on how many people see your ad but don't necessarily click on it (*pay for views*).** If you select the Pay for Views tab, Facebook lets you decide where you want your ad to appear: in people's news feeds (page 78) or in Facebook's ad space (the lower-left part of any screen). If you select Pay for Clicks, Facebook decides where to display your ad.

   In either case, you type in how much you want to pay—per click if you chose the Pay for Clicks route, or per 1,000 impressions if you chose the Pay for Views route. The higher the amount you type in the Bid field, the more often your ad appears (in relation to whatever other ads Facebook needs to run the day yours runs; in other words, the highest bidder gets her ads run more often). Because site traffic and the total number of ads Facebook sells on any given day fluctuate, you also need to type the total amount of money you want to pay Facebook in any 24-hour period in the Budget field. After you tell Facebook which days you want your ad to run, click Continue to preview your ad.

**Note** In the marketing biz, the Pay for Clicks model is known as CPC ("cost per clicks"), and the Pay for Views model is known as CPM ("cost per thousand"—M is the Roman numeral for 1,000).

| 1. Get Started | 2. Choose Audience | 3. Create Ad | 4. Set Budget |

**Price Your Campaign**

| **Pay for Clicks** | Pay for Views | (More information) |

**Budget:** What is the most you want to spend per day? (min $5.00)

$ 5.00

**Bid:** How much are you willing to pay per click? (min $0.01)

$ 0.25

**Schedule:** When do you want to start running your ad?

○ Run my ad continuously starting today

● Start Date: Nov ▼ 21 ▼ , 2007 ▼ at 12:00am PDT

End Date: Nov ▼ 21 ▼ , 2007 ▼ at 11:59pm PDT

Back    Continue ▶

6. **Check your ad for errors, and then enter your credit card informa-tion.** If you spot a mistake, click Change Ad to go back and fix the error. You should check out Facebook's Terms and Conditions, too. Basically, by running your ad, you certify that you're not lying to people or try-ing to sell something objectionable or illegal, like drugs or porn or copyright-protected music. Then head to the bottom of the Review Ad page and click the Place Order button.

**Note** After you create your ad, the only thing you can change about it is whether to pay Facebook per click or per 1,000 impressions. To change what you pay for, head to the Applications menu, click Page Manager, and then click Ad Campaigns.

7. **Check on your ad.** You can see daily statistics as well as in-depth demo-graphics (through Facebook's much-ballyhooed Insights program—see page 190) in as little as a few hours after Facebook starts running your ad. To do so: From the Applications menu, click either Ads, Page Manager, or "Ads and Pages" (the link you see depends on whether you've created an ad, a Page, or both.) Then click the Ad Campaigns tab. To see stats including impressions and clicks broken down by day, click the Daily Stats tab. To see the info in easy-to-interpret graph form, click the Insights tab.

Here's a quickie rundown of the stats you see:

- **Bid ($)** is the amount you bid for this ad (see page 194).

- **CPC** reminds you that you chose to pay on a cost-per-click basis (page 194).

- **Clicks** refers to the number of people who've actually clicked your ad so far.

- **CTR (%)** means "click-through rate"; this is the percentage of the people who've seen your ad who've actually clicked it.

- **Avg. CPC ($)** and **Avg. CPM ($)** show you the amount of money you're spending, on average, per click and per thousand impressions, respectively.

- **Spent ($)** keeps track of how much you've spent on the ad so far based on the amount you bid, the number of clicks or impressions your ad gets, and how many days your ad runs. (If you bought a long-running ad, you can see day-by-day stats by clicking Daily Status.)

To dispense with the columns of numbers and see a chart of how your ad's performing, click Insights.

| Overview | Ad Campaigns | Pages | | | | | | Create an Ad ▶ |
|---|---|---|---|---|---|---|---|---|

**My Ads** rename
Campaign is ▶ **running.** | ▼

**Daily Budget:** $5.00 edit
**Schedule:** 11/21/2007 to 11/21/2007

Stats: ◉ Last 24 hrs ○ Last 7 days ○ All                    Ads | Daily Stats | Insights

| Name | Bid ($) | Type | Imp. | Clicks | CTR (%) | Avg. CPC ($) | Avg. CPM ($) | Spent ($) |
|---|---|---|---|---|---|---|---|---|
| ▶ The Frontera Jazz Quartet | 0.25 | CPC | 18 | 0 | 0.00 | 0.00 | 0.00 | 0.00 |
| Totals | | | 18 | 0 | 0.00 | 0.00 | 0.00 | 0.00 |

Account Billing | Show Deleted Campaigns

# High-dollar Options

Facebook's free-to-inexpensive polls, Pages, and social ads are great for small businesses and freelancers. But companies with a little more dough to throw around can choose from even more advertising options. The following sections explain 'em all.

## Beacon

Facebook's *Beacon* is a brand-spanking-new, still-being-hammered-out program that does for regular Web sites what *social actions* (page 190) do for Facebook Pages. Beacon lets you:

- **Track what people do on your own Web site.** You can track actions like signing up for a service, adding a product to a wish list, and buying something.

- **Create Facebook stories (page 79) about those actions.** "Ralph just added *101 Dalmatians* to his Christmas wish list on CD Zone" is an example of a Facebook story.

- **Combine those stories with an ad and send the whole shebang to all your customers' Facebook friends.** Like the social ads you create all by themselves (page 189) or in conjunction with a Facebook Page (page 182), these customized ads appear both in peoples' news feeds and in the ad space that Facebook reserves on the lower-left side of every screen.

Say you run an online bookstore, and somebody logs in to your site and buys a copy of Upton Sinclair's *The Jungle*. Using Beacon, you can tell whether that somebody is a Facebook member, and if she is, you can send a personalized ad (see the example on page 193) to everyone on her Facebook Friend List. You win in two ways:

- **People are more likely to read your ad if it's coupled with news about someone they know.** It's human nature: We want to know what our friends are up to because we want to learn more about them.

- **Because friends often share tastes and interests, ads you send via Beacon are likely to reach an interested audience.** If someone already visited your site or even bought something from you, the chances that her close friends will follow suit are much higher than if your ad goes out to random people.

Adding Beacon to your Web site involves adding customized code to your site, and it's not cheap. To talk to somebody at Facebook who can walk you through the process: Scroll to the bottom of any Facebook screen and click Businesses; then click Facebook Beacon. On the page that appears, click the Sign Up button; after that, you just wait to hear from somebody on Facebook's sales team.

## Sponsored Marketplace Listings

Chapter 8 showed you how to place free classifieds for products and services in the Facebook Marketplace (page 133). But in addition to free ads, you can pay to have your ad show up on the right side of the Marketplace Home page, complete with a thumbnail picture.

To place a sponsored listing: Scoll to the bottom of any Facebook screen and click Advertisers. Then scroll to the bottom of the page that appears and click the "Contact our sales team" link.

# Sponsored Stories

*Sponsored stories* are the big-business version of *social ads* (page 189). Here's how they work: On the left side of every Facebook member's home page is a News Feed section (page 78). Because most of the gossipy tidbits (a.k.a. "stories"—page 79) that appear in a member's news feed involve that member's close friends, she's likely to actually browse through and read them. So when she comes across a sponsored story sandwiched between news of what her pals are doing, there's a good chance she'll see and even respond to the ad. (By Facebook's estimates, the click-through rate for sponsored stories is 20 times higher than for regular banner ads.) Best of all, a sponsored story can contain lots of text and up to four images or an instantly-playable video clip.

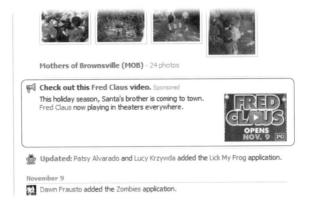

Mothers of Brownsville (MOB) - 24 photos

**Check out this Fred Claus video.** Sponsored
This holiday season, Santa's brother is coming to town.
Fred Claus now playing in theaters everywhere.

**Updated:** Patsy Alvarado and Lucy Krzywda added the Lick My Frog application.

November 9

Dawn Frausto added the Zombies application.

> **Note** Members can't hide their news feeds the way they can hide other sections of their home page—meaning, if they're using Facebook, the only way they can escape seeing a sponsored story is to close their eyes. If you're a marketing type, this is sweet news indeed.

Not surprisingly, it costs big bucks to place a sponsored story: They start at $50,000, at the time of this writing. If you're interested, you need to talk to someone at Facebook to set up the deal (page 257).

> **Tip** To make your message even more meaningful to your audience, consider *sponsored social stories*. A sponsored social story is a regular sponsored story coupled with the news that someone's friend just bought the product (or watched the movie, or became a fan of the Page, or whatever). You create sponsored social stories by adding Beacon (page 197) to your Web site.

## Sponsored Groups

*Sponsored groups* combine the interactivity of regular groups (page 103) with unlimited membership, customized features, and tons of ads. The goal is to make a well-known brand appear as helpful and accessible as the group admin of your Facebook Scrabble group.

**Note** With the advent of Pages (page 182), Facebook plans to phase out sponsored groups over the coming months.

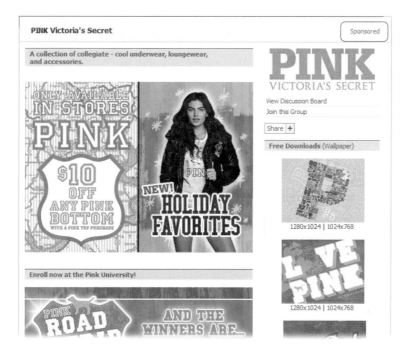

At a starting price of around $300,000, sponsored groups are only for the heaviest of hitters. So it shouldn't come as a surprise that you don't create a sponsored group by filling in a couple of online forms, the way you do a regular group. Instead, you contact Facebook directly (page 257) so your marketing people can work with Facebook to develop a comprehensive marketing strategy.

# 12

# Customizing Facebook and Adding Applications

**F**acebook is a pretty polished-looking site, and it wants to stay that way. Unlike MySpace—where you can customize just about everything on your personal page—you can't go hog-wild changing the way Facebook looks. You can adjust only the layout of your home page and profile ever so slightly. But you *can* do something much cooler than, say, changing the background color of your profile page: Facebook lets you add *applications*—tiny programs that run inside Facebook.

Second only to the friend-to-friend interactions Facebook tracks for you, applications are one of the main reasons for Facebook's explosive popularity. Why? They're fun! And they can be useful, too. Applications let you do everything from silly stuff (such as "spray painting" on your friends' walls or sending your friends virtual potted plants that grow a little each day) to useful things (such as adding chat capability to your Facebook profile or creating a terrific-looking resumé from right inside Facebook).

**Note** Facebook granted programmers free access to the Facebook platform in May of 2007, meaning that for the first time ever, anybody with the programming chops and the desire could create an application. Since then, the number of Facebook applications has skyrocketed. If you can imagine it, somebody's probably created a Facebook application that lets you do it.

As this book goes to press, you can choose from over 10,000 Facebook applications. Read on to learn how to find and install the best of the bunch.

# Modifying Your Home Page and Profile

Facebook gives you a few modest ways to customize the layout of your home page and profile. You can:

- **Collapse and expand sections of your profile.** Click a blue section heading to collapse that section; click it again to expand the section.

**Tip** If a down arrow precedes a section heading, that section is already expanded, so clicking the heading will collapse it. A right arrow means the section is collapsed, so clicking the heading expands it.

▼ Education

Education Info
College:                    Arizona State '90

Click and drag to move this box

▶ Gifts

▶ Information

- **De-emphasize news items and hide sections of your home page.** To de-emphasize a news feed story that's on your home page, head to the right side of the story and click the X. When you do this, the story's text gets really faint and the story gets reduced to one or two lines. The story doesn't disappear completely, but it isn't quite as in-your-face annoying.

**Note** Facebook remembers which stories you de-emphasize and fine-tunes your news feed accordingly. If you really enjoy a certain story, click the thumbs-up icon next to the X to tell Facebook to display more of that kind of news.

show friend

zywda just got messaged.
nd pie to Jessica back or do anything to your friends!

I don't like this

No upcoming birthdays.

rausto got another likeness match.

Invite Your Friends

To remove a section on your home page, click the "hide" link on the right side of the section heading. When you do, Facebook replaces the "hide" link with a "show" link you can click to restore that section.

- **Hide the applications on your profile.** Applications show up on your profile page below your mini-feed (page 80) and personal info, as well as below your profile picture. Clicking the X in an application's blue header displays a pop-up box that lets you choose between hiding the application (you can get it back by editing your applications settings as shown on page 211) or removing it altogether.

- **Reposition sections of your profile.** To do so, mouse over the heading of the section you want to reposition. (Your cursor turns into a four-headed arrow when you're in the right spot.) Then just click and drag to move the section.

# Facebook Applications: An Overview

Facebook *applications* are small programs that work inside Facebook. They're similar to Web browser plug-ins (like video players) in that they let you do a little something extra—something you couldn't do before you installed them. They're easy to install and appear on your Facebook Applications menu.

If you've had a chance to put Facebook through its paces, you're probably already familiar with the site's built-in applications, which include Groups, Events, Photos, and Marketplace. But people who aren't on the Facebook design team—folks known as "third-party developers"—have written about a bazillion others, such as iLike (which lets you add music clips to your profile) and Weekly Schedule (which lets you coordinate a graphic version of your schedule with your co-workers' or friends').

Nearly all the initial third-party Facebook applications are humorous time-wasters, like the ones that let you spray-paint graffiti on someone's wall or hurl virtual sheep at your friends in lieu of a sedate poke (page 66). But you can expect to see more serious-minded, business-friendly applications now that Facebook's enormous (and growing) membership is attracting high-dollar advertisers. Professional Profile, for example, lets you post and edit your resumé on Facebook, then track who views it. Chat-Instant Messaging lets you add an instant-messaging box to your profile so you can communicate with co-workers without ever leaving Facebook.

Facebook applications are super easy to find, install, and use. The only downside to using them is that you automatically grant the application's developers access to your profile, which poses a security risk. Flip to page 214 to learn more.

> **Note** If you're interested in creating a Facebook application of your own, check out *http://developers.facebook.com* for details on the newly released Facebook development platform. (You can get to that site by scrolling to the bottom of any Facebook screen and clicking the Developers link.) And for a business-minded analysis of the application market, check out *The Facebook Application Platform: An O'Reilly Radar Report* (*http://radar.oreilly.com/research/reports/facebook.html*).

# Finding Applications

Facebook's application directory lets you search for applications by category or popularity, or see a list of the newest ones. To find applications:

1. **Head to the Applications menu and click either the Applications link or the "edit" link next to it.** Then, on the Edit My Applications page that appears, click the Browse More Applications button.

2. **Browse the applications.** If you know what you're looking for—something that might make college life easier or more fun, for example—head to the right-hand column and choose a category such as Education. If you're curious which applications people are using or which ones are hot off the press, click one of the tabs at the top of the page: Recently Popular, Most Activity, Most Active Users, or Newest.

**Tip** If you know the name of the application you're looking for, type it in the Search Apps field and hit Return.

# Adding Applications

You have to install Facebook applications before you can use them, but installing them is a snap:

1. **In the Application Directory, click the name of the application you want to install.** Up pops a page with more info about the application.

**Tip** Here's another way to add applications: When you're browsing a friend's profile and see an interesting application, click the "add" link on the application's blue header. Then jump to step 3 below.

2. **Click the Add Application button.**

3. **On the confirmation page that appears, decide how much of your personal info you want to share with the application.** You can turn off all the checkboxes except "Know who I am and access my information" (turn that one off, and Facebook won't let you install the application).

**Tip** Leave one or both of the "Place a link" checkboxes turned on so you can find the application easily after you install it.

**Add FunWall to your Facebook account?**

**FunWall**
by Slide, Inc.

**The Developer's Description**

" Add some FUN to your Wall! Let your friends post photos, videos, slap funny pictures on pictures -- and more! -- on this replacement for the boring original.

More Information about FunWall

Allow this application to...

☑ Know who I am and access my information
☑ Put a box in my profile
☑ Place a link in my left-hand navigation
☑ Publish stories in my News Feed and Mini-Feed
☑ Place a link below the profile picture on any profile

FunWall was **not created by Facebook**. By clicking 'add,' you agree to the Platform Application Terms of Use.

**→] Add FunWall** or Cancel

Afraid of abuse by this application?
Block FunWall

---

**Note** You can add some applications to your Facebook Pages (page 182)—if you have any—in addition to adding them to your profile. On the confirmation page, you'll see separate "Add to Profile" and "Add to Page" buttons.

4. **Click the Add button.** Facebook installs the application and displays it so you can start using it right away.

# Using Applications

The way you use an application and the things you can do with it completely depend on the application itself. But the way you *open* an application so you can use it is always the same: Head to the Applications menu and click the name of the application you want to use. (Alternatively, you can head to your profile and click either the application's icon that appears under your profile picture, or the blue link that appears in the section of your profile dedicated to that application (the wording of the link depends on the application).

Wherever you find the application link, as soon as you click it, Facebook displays the application, all ready to go.

> **Tip** If you chose not to display the application on your profile or in your Applications menu (see page 211), you can still use the application. To do so, scroll to the Applications menu and click the "edit" link. Then, on the Edit My Applications page, click the name of the application you want to use.

# Troubleshooting Applications

If an application doesn't behave the way you expect it to, you've got a couple of options: You can delete the application (see page 213) or check to see if there's a help or Frequently Asked Questions page. If there's not a help page, or if the FAQ doesn't answer your question, you can contact the folks who created the application. Here's how to check for a help page and contact an application's creator:

1. **Scroll to the bottom of any Facebook screen and click the bottom-right Help link.**

2. **Scroll to the bottom of the Help Topics screen.** In the Added Applications section, click the name of the application you need help with.

3. **In the Help box that appears, click the "help page" link (if one exists).** If there isn't a help page for the application or if you read the help page and it doesn't help, type your question or feedback in the Your Message text box and click Send.

---

**Help For FunWall**

Have you first looked at the help page for FunWall?

The information you provide below will be automatically submitted to the creator of **FunWall**. If you would like a response, please provide an email address.

|  |  |
|---|---|
| To: | FunWall |
| Your Email: | [                    ] |
|  | **Not required.** The application developer will receive this email address. Only provide if you need a response. |
| Subject: | [                    ] |
| Your Message: | [                    ] |

[ Send ]  [ Cancel ]

---

# Controlling Where Applications Appear and Who Knows You're Using Them

When you first add an application, Facebook gives you the opportunity to tell it where you want the application to appear: on your Applications menu, for example, or on your profile as either a section, or as a tiny icon beneath your profile picture. (See page 213.)

But you can change your mind at any time and, for example, tell Facebook to stop displaying an application on your profile. In addition, you can tell Facebook whether or not you want the site to announce what you do with the application on your mini-feed and in your friends' news feeds.

To change where an application appears and who gets to know you're using it:

1. **Head to the Applications menu and click the "edit" link.**

**Edit My Applications**

Use this page to control which applications appear on your profile, application menu, or News Feed. You can change your preferences at any time. You can change your applications' privacy settings from the Privacy page.

Browse More Applications ▶

| | | | |
|---|---|---|---|
| 🎯 **Ads and Pages** (about) | Edit Settings | | ✕ Remove |
| 📅 **Events** (about) | Edit Settings | | ✕ Remove |
| 💬 **FunWall** (about) | Edit Settings | Profile, News Feed, Mini-Feed, profile links disabled | ✕ Remove |
| 🎁 **Gifts** (about) | Edit Settings | Left menu disabled | ✕ Remove |
| 👥 **Groups** (about) | Edit Settings | | ✕ Remove |
| 🎵 **iLike** (about) | Edit Settings | | ✕ Remove |
| 🛒 **Marketplace** (about) | Edit Settings | | ✕ Remove |
| 📱 Mobile (about) | Edit Settings | | ✕ Remove |

2. **On the Edit My Applications page that appears, find the name of the application you want and click Edit Settings.**

**Edit Settings For iLike**

| | |
|---|---|
| Profile: | All my networks and all my friends . ▼ |
| Left Menu: | ☑ Show this in my left-hand menu. |
| News Feed: | ☑ Publish stories about this in my News Feed. |
| Mini-Feed: | ☑ Publish stories about this in my Mini-Feed. |
| Profile Links: | ☑ Add a link below the profile picture to any profile. |
| Email: | ☑ Allow this application to contact me via email. |
| Other: | Other privacy settings |

Save   Cancel

3. **In the Edit Settings box that appears, tell Facebook where to display your application, and who to tell about it.** Most of the options are pretty clearly described for you, but two are a little confusing. Choosing any selection other than "No one" from the Profile drop-down list adds a section to your profile similar to the one you see on the next page. Checking the Profile Links checkbox adds a tiny icon to the row of icons that appears right below your Profile picture.

> **Tip** Not all applications offer additional settings, but some do. If you see the Other Privacy Settings link, *click it*. Doing so lets you control what kinds of additional things—such as links and even other applications—the application can display on your profile.

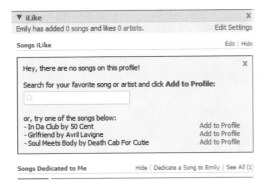

## Deleting Applications

If you decide you don't like an application or just find it takes up too much real estate on your Applications menu or profile, you can delete it quickly and easily:

1. **Head to the Applications menu and click the "edit" link.**

2. **On the Edit My Applications page that appears, find the name of the application you want to delete and click the Remove link.** In the confirmation box that appears, click Remove.

If you change your mind and want to use the application again, simply reinstall it (page 208).

> **Tip** To hide your application without deleting it, edit your application settings. Page 211 shows you how.

## Customizing Your Applications Menu

Unless you tell it otherwise (page 211), Facebook lists all your applications (in the order you installed them) on the Applications menu, with the built-in Facebook applications at the top of the list. But you can reorder the list. You might want to do this if you find yourself using one application more than the others and want it at the top of your Applications menu. To reorder your Applications menu:

1. **Head to the Applications menu and click either Applications or the "edit" link.** Facebook puts a four-headed arrow in front of each of your application listings.

2. **Click and drag the four-headed arrow next to the listing you want to move.** When you've put the listing where you want it, let go of your mouse.

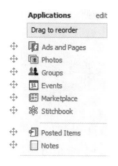

 Instead of clicking and dragging the arrow, you can click and drag the application link itself.

3. **Get rid of the arrows.** When you finish rearranging your Applications menu, click anywhere else on the screen (for example, the Facebook logo ) to redisplay the menu with clickable links—and no arrows.

## Applications and Privacy

Before you can install an application, you have to agree to give that application's creators access to all—yes, *all*—the personal info you've typed into Facebook (that's what the "Know who I am and access my information" checkbox means—see step 3 on page 208). What's more, Facebook isn't responsible if these folks use your personal information for nefarious purposes, lose it, sell it, or write it across the sky in 200-foot-high letters. That's a scary thought—especially if you've added your home address, credit card info, or other super-sensitive details to your Facebook account.

Chapter 13 discusses privacy in detail, and you really, really ought to read it. But the upshot is this: When deciding whether you want to share your info, think about how much sensitive stuff you've typed into Facebook, how bad off you'd be if it fell into the wrong hands, and how useful you find the application you want to install.

# 13

# Playing It Safe: Facebook Privacy

S ocial networking sites like Facebook depend on millions of people voluntarily divulging accurate personal information. But in a world where identity theft is a growing concern and spammers can't wait to get their hands on your email address, how do you take advantage of what Facebook has to offer while minimizing risks to your personal info? This chapter explains Facebook's privacy issues, and then gives you strategies for staying safe—from up-front planning to adjusting Facebook's privacy settings to after-the-fact damage control.

# Privacy and Facebook: An Overview

If you're connected to the Internet, privacy is a concern. Surf the Web—privacy risk. Use email—privacy risk. The sad truth is that there are a lot of bad guys out there, and your personal info is worth a lot of money to some of them. Even virus protection and firewalls can't always keep bad things from happening to you. And while Facebook promises to do all it can to protect the personal data you add to your profile, mistakes happen. In fact, Facebook's privacy policy clearly states that anything you disclose on the site "may become publicly available," and that all members agree to use the site "at their own risk." Gulp.

> **Note:** To read Facebook's privacy policy, head to the bottom of any Facebook screen and click the Privacy link.

The trick is to balance the benefits you get from using Facebook (and the Internet in general) with the risk of losing control of your private information.

> **Note:** If you're like most people, your personal information is already stored in lots of databases (your bank's, your favorite magazine's, and so on). But what's unique about Facebook's cache of personal data is that it includes intimate details (like your views on politics, religion, and relationships), and that it's tied to a *picture* of you (your profile picture—page 15). This combination of identifying details with a visual image is one of the things that makes Facebook so interesting and compelling—but also so potentially dangerous. Theoretically, someone could find out what town you live in and where you plan to be next Tuesday at 8:00 p.m. (a book club meeting you RSVP'd to on Facebook, for example). Armed with your picture, that someone could show up at your book club and try to convince you he's your long-lost cousin Al who's down on his luck and needs a couple thousand to tide him over.

## Privacy Threats

Some of the privacy threats associated with Facebook are the same that many online companies face, such as recent reports that the Facebook source code (the raw programming that powers the site) was leaked onto the Internet, potentially giving hackers access to Facebook members' personal information. And, of course, any info you send via the Internet is vulnerable to interception. But there are other Facebook-specific threats, too:

- **Third-party application developers and other Facebook partners.** Before you can use a Facebook application, you have to grant the person or company who created the application access to your personal data (see page 214). Once you grant that access, control of your personal info is out of Facebook's hands: If the application's creator misuses your information, the beef is between you and them. Likewise, Facebook's privacy policy lets the site share your personal details with companies who advertise or sell products on Facebook, and it's up to those firms to keep your data safe.

- **People you didn't think had access to your profile.** If you think only people who live in your city, attended your alma mater, or work at your company can view your profile, you're wrong. Hiring managers, parents, teachers, police officers, and other folks who are determined to view your Facebook profile can find a way to do so—either by asking a co-worker or friend who happens to be a member of your Facebook network to look up your information, or (in the case of cops) by getting a court order.

- **Anybody using a search engine.** Depending on the privacy levels you set in Facebook, anybody can search your profile information using a garden-variety search engine such as Yahoo.com, even if the person's not a Facebook member.

> **Note:** Because many of Facebook's privacy levels are opt out (meaning Facebook assumes you want the whole world to see your personal info until you tell it differently), your information is at risk until you adjust your settings as shown in this chapter.

## Strategies for Keeping Your Info Private

So that's the bad news. The *good* news is that just three simple strategies give you quite a bit of control when it comes to keeping your private data safe:

- **Don't put sensitive info on Facebook.** You get to choose what kind of information you share with the site, and how much. Data thieves can't steal your Social Security number, for example, if you don't make it available.

- **Customize your privacy settings.** Much as keeping your front door locked dramatically reduces the chance of being robbed, customizing your privacy settings minimizes—but does *not* eliminate—the chance of your Facebook data falling into the wrong hands. Starting on page 222, this chapter shows you which settings can help protect your privacy.

- **If the worst happens, fight back.** If a spurned lover tracks you down on Facebook and starts harassing you, you can shut her down by blocking her access to your Facebook profile (page 236) or reporting her to Facebook (page 237).

# Deciding How Much to Share

How confessional you want to be when you create your Facebook profile is entirely up to you. But here are a few things to consider:

- **Give Facebook only enough info to get what you want out of the site.** If you're looking to connect with other early music fans, for example, limit your profile info to medieval subjects. If you plan to use Facebook to find parenting tips, don't feel you have to share your academic and work backgrounds.

- **Consider keeping your public and private identities separate.** If you're planning to use Facebook primarily for networking, think twice about posting pictures of your wild weekend in Jamaica. You don't have to forego mentions of your personal life completely, but you should limit your personal info to the kind of thing you'd feel comfortable tacking up on your cubicle wall.

- **Think about creating an email address just for Facebook.** Companies such as Google and Yahoo let you create a free Web-based email address you can use to sign up for Facebook. Using an email address dedicated to Facebook protects your "real" work or home email address from accidental or deliberate theft (think: spammers).

- **If it's sensitive and optional, leave it out.** Random people viewing your profile don't need to know your home address or phone number. If you meet people on Facebook and want to share this information with them, you can always do so in a more private way (such as a Facebook message—page 60).

- **When in doubt, do the "mom or boss" check.** If you'd be comfortable telling your mom or your boss something, go ahead and post it on your profile. Otherwise, skip it.

# Controlling Access to Your Account

While you need to be wary of people getting access to your account info online, don't forget to take precautions in the real world, too: Make sure no one can log in to Facebook as you. You already know not to share your password with anyone, but there are a couple other steps you should take to protect your account. To prevent co-workers, fellow students, or family members from using your computer to access your Facebook account (either by accident or design), follow these steps:

1. **Log in the smart way.** After you type your email address and Face-book password into the login page (*www.facebook.com/login.php*), make sure the "Remember me" checkbox is turned *off* before you click the Login button.

**facebook**

Email:
eamoore68@gmail.com

Password:
•••••••

☐ Remember me

Login

Forgot Password?

2. **Log out when you're finished using Facebook.** Before you go on to the next item on your to-do list, take a second to click the "logout" link in the upper-right corner of every Facebook screen. Doing so prevents people from getting into your account if you forget to close your browser before you head out for lunch.

# Adjusting Your Privacy Settings

Facebook does a lot of media chest-thumping about how strictly it protects its members' privacy. So, it may come as a surprise that, unless you change them, *your privacy settings are set to the slackest possible levels.* It's up to you to understand how Facebook's privacy settings work, where to find them, how to adjust them—and to actually spend time battening down the hatches. That's a lot of work! Fortunately, this book has done most of the work for you; all you have to do is read this section and adjust your settings.

> **Note** In a privacy study reported recently in a British newspaper, 41 percent of Facebook members chose to befriend (page 45) a plastic frog, thereby granting the fictitious "Freddi Staur" (an anagram for "ID Fraudster") access to personal details such as their home addresses, children's names, and family photo albums. The moral? Don't befriend indiscriminately on Facebook any more than you would offline.

## Controlling Who Sees Your Profile and Contact Info

You can make your entire profile off-limits to certain groups of people, such as the people in one of your networks. You can also hide specific parts of your profile—like your contact information and which applications you've added—from whole groups of people, such as one of your networks or all your friends. To do so:

1. **At the top right of any Facebook screen, click the "privacy" link.**

2. **On the Privacy Overview page that appears, click Profile**.

---

**Privacy Overview**

Facebook wants you to share your information with exactly the people you want to see it. On this page, you'll find all the controls you need to set who can see your profile and the stuff in it, who can find and contact you on Facebook, and more.

**Profile**
You are in one network and you can control who can see your profile, contact information, groups, wall, photos, posted items, online status, and status updates.
Edit Settings

**Search**
You can control who can find you in searches and what appears in your search listing.
Edit Settings

**News Feed and Mini-Feed**
You can control what actions show up in your Mini-Feed and your friends' News Feeds.
Edit Settings

**Poke, Message, and Friend Request**
You can select which parts of your profile are visible to people you contact through a poke, message, or friend request.
Edit Settings

**Applications**
You can edit your privacy for applications you have added to your account, applications that you have used on another website, and other applications built on Facebook Platform.
Edit Settings

**External Websites**
You can edit your privacy settings for external websites sending stories to your profile.
Edit Settings

**Block People**

If you block someone, they will not be able to search for you, see your profile, or contact you on Facebook. Any ties you currently have with a person you block will be broken (friendship connections, relationships, etc).

Person:

**Limited Profile**

If you want to hide some of the information in your profile from specific people, add them to your limited profile list below.
Edit Settings

Person: _____ [Add]

---

**Note** The line graphs to the right of each category on the Privacy Overview page—Profile, Search, and so on—give you a visual cue of how private Facebook thinks your data is. (The longer the line, the less private your data is.) To edit a category's privacy settings, click the name of the category, the Edit Settings link next to the category, or the category's line.

3. **On the "Privacy Settings for your Profile" page that appears, use the drop-down lists to control who can see your profile, your Friend List, your contact information, and more.** It's a big page, so there are lots of settings to adjust. But all the options are pretty much the same, and Facebook breaks down the settings into three basic categories to make it easier for you to decide which option you want for each setting:

- **Profile.** Here's where you grant access to your profile page. If you want long-lost friends and co-workers to be able to look you up, keep the "All my networks and all my friends" setting that Facebook starts you out with. Choose "Some of my networks," for the Profile field, and Facebook lets you choose which network(s) you want to grant access to. Choosing "Only my friends" keeps Facebook members who aren't on your Friend List from seeing your profile. To restrict access to specific parts of your profile (like the Friends and Wall sections), head to the fields below the Profile field and adjust each section's setting separately.

**Privacy Settings for your Profile**

Based on your **current** privacy settings, people from Rio Grande Valley, TX, and all your friends can see your profile. Your profile may include your picture, interests, photo albums, groups, wall and other things, depending on the profile details you have selected.

Back to Privacy Overview without saving changes.

**Profile**

You can control who can see your profile — your **friends** can always see your profile, and you can allow **all your networks** or **some of your networks** to see your profile.

Profile: | All my networks and all my friends ▼ |————•

You can also control who can see each **profile feature**. Only people who can see your **profile** can see this information. Read more about these settings.

Status Updates: | All my networks and all my friends ▼ |————•
☑ Allow friends to subscribe to my status updates

Videos Tagged of You: | All my networks and all my friends ▼ |————•
Photos Tagged of You: | All my networks and all my friends ▼ |————•
Online Status: | All my networks and all my friends ▼ |————•
Friends: | All my networks and all my friends ▼ |————•
Wall: | All my networks and all my friends ▼ |————•
All my networks and all my friends
Some of my networks and all my friends
Only my friends
Only me

**Contact Information**
No one

You can control who can see your contact [information...] your contact information, and you can allow **all your networks** or **some of your networks** to see your contact information. Only people who can see your **profile** can see your contact information.

- **Contact Information.** This section lets you control who gets to see non-Facebook ways to contact you, like your phone number, address, and instant messaging screen name. Adjust all these settings to "Only my friends" unless you have a darn good reason not to (if, for example, you signed up with Facebook because you're coordinating your high school reunion and want far-flung former classmates to be able to contact you). Consider choosing "No one" from the "contact emails" drop-down list (or lists, if you've given Facebook more than one email address) to prevent folks you don't know from clogging your personal or work email account with spam.

> **Tip** You get to choose who sees your personal Web site (if you have one) in the Profile section, too; in most cases, you'll want to select the "All my networks and all my friends" option for this setting.

- **Applications in your Profile.** This section lets you decide who can see the applications you've installed. (You might want to prevent your boss from seeing that you've installed an application to help you find a new job, for example.) Most applications offer the same privacy options as you set for your profile and contact info, but some—including the built-in Photos and Notes applications—offer additional settings. For example, you can set different privacy levels for each of the albums you create using Photos. To control access to an application, click either the drop-down list beside the application's name, or the application's name beside the blue padlock icon.

You can control who can see the **applications** added to your **profile**. Only people who can see your **profile** can see these **applications**. Click on items that have a 🔒 to access their privacy page.

🔒 **Photos:** (Privacy settings available on another page)
🔒 **Notes:** (Privacy settings available on another page)
Posted Items: No one ▾
Groups: All my networks and all my friends ▾

4. **When you finish adjusting your privacy settings, scroll to the bottom of the page and click the Save button.**

# Creating a Stripped-down Profile

In addition to controlling what profile info certain groups of people—such as network members or friends—can see (page 224), you can create a stripped-down, *limited profile* to show specific Facebook members.

> **Note** Confusingly, Facebook lets you create a second stripped-down version of your profile to show to people you poke, message, or attempt to befriend. See page 230 for details.

A limited profile is useful if you know someone's a Facebook member and you don't want her to know certain things about you. Say you're expecting a hiring manager to look you up on Facebook and want to hide your slightly-inappropriate notes, or you don't want an annoyingly clinging co-worker to know which groups you're a member of and which events you plan to attend.

> **Note** You can substitute your limited profile for your "real" profile for any Facebook member, whether or not she's in one of your networks or on your Friend List.

To create and use a limited profile:

1. **At the top right of any Facebook screen, click the "privacy" link.**

2. **On the Privacy Overview page that appears, scroll down to the Limited Profile section and click Edit Settings.** Then, on the Limited Profile Settings page, turn off the checkboxes next to the profile sections you want to hide from certain individuals. Because you can't create different limited profiles for different people, consider turning off all the checkboxes. (Hey—better safe than sorry.)

## Limited Profile Settings

You can hide some of the information in your **profile** from specific people by changing your limited profile settings and creating a list of people that only see your limited profile. You can choose to include Mini-Feed in your limited profile, and you can select which photo albums you want to show.

Back to Privacy Overview without saving changes.

### Information

Select the information to display in your limited profile.

- [ ] Basic Info
- [ ] Contact Info
- [ ] Personal Info
- [ ] Education Info
- [ ] Work Info
- [ ] Wall
- [ ] Photos Tagged of Me
- [ ] Videos Tagged of Me
- [ ] Online Status
- [ ] Status Updates
- [ ] Friends
- [ ] Posted Items
- [ ] Notes
- [ ] Groups

### Preview

The preview below shows what your profile will look like to people on your limited profile list.

### Limited Profile List

List the people who you want to see your limited profile instead of your full profile.

**Person:** [_____] [ Add ]

---

**Note** You can also prevent your mini-feed and specific photo albums from appearing on your limited profile. To do so, scroll down to the bottom of the Limited Profile Settings page and turn off the checkboxes next to Mini-Feed and each photo album you want to hide.

---

### Mini-Feed

By selecting the checkbox below, you can include Mini-Feed in your limited profile. If you choose to keep Mini-Feed in your limited profile, only the items you selected in the information section above will be included in your Mini-Feed.

- [ ] Mini-Feed

### Photo Albums

Select which albums you want to show in your limited profile.

- [ ] "Acme Photography--Little Miss RGV account"

[ Save ] [ Cancel ]

3. **Tell Facebook who you want to show your limited profile to (versus your full profile).** On the Limited Profile Settings page, click the Person field and start typing a name. As soon as you do, Facebook displays a list of people on your Friend List who match what you've typed in. If you spot the name of the person you want to add, simply click the name to select it, and then click the Add button.

   If you type a name that isn't on your Friend List, Facebook changes the Add button to a Search button. Click Search to display a list of Facebook members whose names match what you typed in. When you spot the correct name in the search results, click the Limited Profile Access link to the right of the member's picture. Bingo: The next time that person tries to access your Facebook profile, they see your limited profile instead.

**Note** You can do a preemptive strike, if you like, by granting someone limited access to your profile *before* they get a chance to look you up on Facebook. You can do this if you want to shield details from, say, a boss, parent, or ex-spouse.

## Hiding from Facebook and Web Searches

Unless you tell it otherwise, Facebook shows your name and profile picture to everyone who looks you up using Facebook's search feature (page 36)—and lets them poke, message, and befriend you—as well as to any non-Facebook member who looks you up using a search engine such as Google. Big deal, right? Letting folks find you and contact you is the reason most people join Facebook, after all.

Actually, it *is* a big deal. If someone pokes you and you poke back—or sends you a message and you respond to it, or sends you a friend request and you accept it—*Facebook automatically grants that person temporary access to your profile, even if he's neither a friend nor a fellow network member.*

**Note** Blocking someone (page 236) prevents them from seeing your profile or interacting with you on Facebook in any way.

If the thought of unintentionally granting profile access to people you don't know makes you a little nervous, you've got three choices:

- **Tell Facebook not to display your name or picture in non-friends' search results.** This is a good choice if you're not interested in long-lost friends or potential employers looking you up, but instead joined Facebook to keep in touch with people you already know. To choose this option: At the top of any Facebook page, click the "privacy" link. On the Privacy Overview page that appears, click Search. Finally, from the "Which Facebook users can find me in search?" drop-down list, choose "Only my friends". (When you do, the "My public search listing" setting disappears.) To confirm your changes, scroll to the bottom of the screen and click the Save button.

**Note** To keep people (including non-Facebook members) from looking you up using Google or some other search engine, head to the "Create a public search listing for me and submit it for search engine indexing" checkbox and uncheck it. (Just for fun, before you turn off the checkbox, click the "see preview" link to check out the bare-bones listing that Facebook *would* have shown searchers based on the "What Can People Do with My Search Results" options you set. Non-Facebook members can see that you're on Facebook, but they can't see your full profile or contact you until they sign up for Facebook.)

---

**Privacy Settings for Search**

You will show up in search results if anyone searches for "**emily moore**" or any part of your name. Even though anyone can search for you, only your friends and everyone from Rio Grande Valley, TX, can see your profile. In addition, people in college networks, high school networks, company networks, regional networks and no networks can see you in search results. People who can't see your profile can see your profile picture, poke you, message you and send you a friend request from your search listing.

Back to Privacy Overview without saving changes.

**Who Can Find Me in Search and See My Public Search Listing**

You can allow **everyone** on Facebook to find you in search results, including browse and group members list, or you can select **restricted** settings to allow only certain people from inside and **outside** your networks to find you in search results. Your friends can always find you in search results.

> **Which Facebook users can find me in search?**
> Everyone ▾ |——————|
>
> **My public search listing**
> ☑ Create a public search listing for me and submit it for search engine indexing (see preview)

**In addition** to the people selected above, allow the following people outside your networks to find you in search results:

☑ People in college networks
☑ People in high school networks
☑ People in company networks
☑ People in regional networks
☑ People with no networks

- **Pare down the information that appears in peoples' search results.** For example, you can tell Facebook not to include your picture, or not to let people poke you or see who your friends are. This option lets you connect with long-lost friends while minimizing the risk of showing too much profile info to people you don't know. Here's what you do: At the top of any Facebook page, click the "privacy" link. On the Privacy Overview page that appears, click Search. On the "Privacy Settings for Search" page, scroll down until you see the What Can People Do With My Search Results section, and turn off the checkboxes next to the items you don't want to appear in people's search results. (Consider turning off all the checkboxes *except* "See your picture" and "Send you a message".) When you finish, click Save.

**Note** "Search results" applies both to people searching for you from within Facebook, and people searching for you using Yahoo or some other search engine.

People in company networks
☑ People in regional networks
☑ People with no networks

**What Can People Do With My Search Results**

You can choose what is in your search listing. People who can see your profile are allowed to do all of the actions below. For people who can't see your profile, select what they can do. **Note:** These settings also apply to your public search listing, but only people who are logged in to Facebook will be able to take any of these actions.

☑ See your picture
☑ Send you a message
☑ Poke you
☑ Add you as a friend
☑ View your friend list

Save    Cancel

- **Customize the profile Facebook shows to non-friend, non-fellow-network-member Facebook members you poke, message, or send friend requests to.** Choose this option if you want to let people look you up out of the blue, but still want to keep some profile details private until you've formalized your relationship. Here's how: At the top of any Facebook page, click the "privacy" link. On the Privacy Overview page that appears, click "Poke, Message, and Friend Request". On the settings page that appears, scroll down to the Information section and turn off the checkboxes next to the stuff you don't want to show casual contacts. (Consider turning off all the checkboxes *except* Basic Info.)

**Poke, Message and Friend Request Settings**

When you contact someone through a **poke**, **message**, o
profile temporarily, even if your privacy and network setting
This helps that person identify who you are before they res
using the check boxes below.

Back to Privacy Overview without saving changes.

**Information**

Select the information to display in your **profile** to the
people that you contact through a poke, message, or
friend request.

- ☑ Basic Info
- ☐ Contact Info
- ☑ Personal Info
- ☑ Education Info
- ☑ Work Info
- ☐ Wall
- ☑ Photos Tagged of Me
- ☑ Videos Tagged of Me
- ☐ Online Status
- ☐ Status Updates
- ☑ Friends
- ☐ Posted Items
- ☐ Notes
- ☐ Groups

[ Save ]   [ Cancel ]

# Controlling Automatic Feeds

Other Facebook members can see what you're up to by visiting the Mini-Feed section of your profile (page 80), and by requesting automatic news feeds detailing your Facebook activities (page 84). To control what kinds of information appear on those feeds:

1. **At the top of any Facebook page, click the "privacy" link.**

2. **On the Privacy Overview page that appears, click "News Feed and Mini-Feed".** On the "News Feed and Mini-Feed Privacy" page that appears, turn off the checkboxes next to categories you want to hide from friends' news feeds and from the mini-feed that appears on your profile. (Remember: Everyone who can see your profile can read your mini-feed). When you're finished, click the Save Changes button.

**News Feed and Mini-Feed Privacy**

Back to Privacy Overview without saving changes

Facebook will only publish stories about you on your Mini-Feed and in the News Feeds of your friends.

Stories are published when you edit your profile information, join a new network, or update your Status. Also publish stories when you...

- ☑ Remove Profile Info
- ☑ Write a Wall Post
- ☑ Comment on a Note
- ☑ Comment on a Photo
- ☑ Comment on a Video
- ☑ Comment on a Posted Item
- ☑ Post on a Discussion Board
- ☑ Add a Friend
- ☑ Remove my Relationship Status
- ☑ Leave a Group
- ☑ Leave a Network

Have something you'd like to see here?

Mini-Feed can show the time when stories were published.

- ☑ Show times in my Mini-Feed

[ Save Changes ] [ Cancel ]

# Deciding What Applications Can Access

You can't use a third-party Facebook application without granting the application access to your profile information (see page 214). And if you're friends with someone who installed a Facebook application, *that* application has access to your profile information, too. But you do have a little bit of control over how Facebook applications use your data:

- **In some cases, you can limit how people can interact with the applications you've installed.** If you put together a photo album using the Photo application (page 163), for example, you can hide the album from certain networks. Or, if you've created a bunch of blog entries using the Notes application (page 90), you can tell Facebook who gets to comment on your notes. Your ability to restrict access to an application depends on the specific application.

- **You can limit the profile info that Facebook routes to your friends' applications.** When your friends install applications, those apps lead straight to you. You can't keep your friends' applications from learning who you are (and who *your* friends are), but you *can* hide other profile details.

To limit how you friends and fellow network members can interact with the applications you've installed:

1. **At the top of any Facebook page, click the "privacy" link.**

2. **On the Privacy Overview page that appears, choose Applications.**

3. **On the Added Applications tab that appears, scroll down to the application whose privacy settings you want to adjust and click the "privacy settings" link.** The settings page that appears depends on the application. For example, the Notes application lets you specify who can see your notes, comment on them, and subscribe to them. The Photos application lets you adjust privacy settings for each of your photo albums individually. (If an application doesn't have a "privacy settings" link *and* it's not a built-in application whose privacy you can control via your profile settings [see page 224], you can't adjust its settings. In that case, if you don't like the way the application behaves, your only option is to remove it.)

To limit the amount of your personal info that Facebook supplies to your friends' applications:

1. **At the top of any Facebook page, click the "privacy" link.**

2. **On the Privacy Overview page that appears, choose Applications.** Then click the Other Applications tab.

Added Applications  Authorized Applications  **Other Applications**

### Privacy Settings for Other Applications

Applications may be able to access a limited set of information about you through friends who opt in to other applications. You can restrict what information is available to these other applications.

**Please note:**

- **Facebook does not sell your information.**
- Your contact information is not exposed by the Facebook Platform.
- Applications that you opt into are not subject to the privacy settings below.
- Your other Facebook privacy settings combine with these settings. Explain more

Back to Privacy Overview without saving changes.

### What Other Users Can See via the Facebook Platform

The following settings apply only to Facebook Platform applications to which you have not already granted access or explicitly restricted. For these applications, the information you select will be available to friends and other users who can already see your information on Facebook.

- ◉ Share my name, networks, and list of friends, as well as the following information:

☑ Profile picture                                      ☑ Groups you belong to
☑ Basic info  What's this?                             ☑ Events you're invited to
☑ Personal info (activities, interests, etc.)          ☑ Photos taken by you
☑ Current location (what city you're in)               ☑ Photos taken of you
☑ Education history                                    ☑ Relationship status

3. **Turn off the checkboxes next to the things you want to hide from your friends' applications.** You probably want to turn off every single one, unless you think your friends would enjoy knowing you use a certain application. (Sometimes it's fun to be the one who "discovers" a great application that's so addictive that everybody you know starts using it!) When you're finished, scroll to the bottom of the page and click Save.

**Note** Another way to limit what your friends' applications can see about you is to *block* an application. Blocking prevents that application from getting *any* information about you. To block an application: In the Application Directory (click Applications, and then click the Browse More Applications button), select the name of the application you want to block. Then, on the application page that appears, click the Block Application link.

## Controlling Who Learns What You're Up To

Facebook's newly announced Beacon program (page 197) lets big Web sites track what you do on their sites, and then shoot out custom ads to your Facebook friends based on what you did. ("Fred just bought high-top tennis shoes from our site. Want a pair?")

When you interact with one of Facebook's Beacon-ized partners—say you surf to the site and buy something or sign up for a service—the site gives you the opportunity to "opt out" of letting the site announce your actions to your Facebook friends. But in addition to notifying your friends, the site may choose to display the news on your profile—and you can control *that* behavior through Facebook.

> **Note** Whether and how external Web sites should give you the ability to opt out of Beacon is currently the topic of heated discussion. The Beacon feature will probably undergo some changes in the coming months.

To control which external Web sites can package up news of your interactions with them and post it on your Facebook profile:

1. **At the top of any Facebook page, click the "privacy" link.**

2. **On the Privacy Overview page that appears, choose External Websites.**

3. **On the "Privacy Settings for External Websites" page, choose which sites you want to let advertise your activities.** If you see a list of Web sites, Facebook displays a "Don't allow any websites to send stories to my profile" checkbox next to each one that you can use to prevent sites from announcing your activities. Simply turn on the checkbox for each site you want to restrict, and then click Save.

---

**Privacy Settings for External Websites**
Back to Privacy Overview without saving changes.

Show your friends what you like and what you're up to outside of Facebook. When you take actions on the sites listed below, you can choose to have those actions sent to your profile.

Please note that these settings only affect notifications on Facebook. You will still be notified on affiliate websites when they send stories to Facebook. You will be able to decline individual stories at that time.

**No sites have tried sending stories to your profile. When they do, those sites will appear in a list on this page.**

☐ Don't allow any websites to send stories to my profile.

[ Save ] [ Cancel ]

---

# Fighting Back

If you're being harassed by another Facebook member—someone fills your wall with unsavory comments, for example, or sends you threatening messages, or pokes you fifty times a day—you can take action. The first thing you want to do is stop your tormentor from contacting you on Facebook. If that doesn't do the trick, you can take self-defense a step further and report the person to Facebook.

## Blocking Individual Members

Facebook lets you prevent individual members from knowing that you're even on the site. *Blocking* someone keeps him from seeing your profile, finding you with Facebook searches, or contacting you via Facebook. To block someone:

> **Note** To prevent people who aren't on Facebook from using a search engine like Google to see that you're on Facebook, you have to tell Facebook *not* to create a public search listing for you (see page 228).

1. **At the top of any Facebook page, click the "privacy" link.**

2. **On the Privacy Overview page that appears, scroll down to the Block People section and, in the Person field, type the name of the member you want to block.** Then click Search.

**Block People**

If you block someone, they will not be able to search you, see your profile, or contact you on Facebook. A ties you currently have with a person you block will b broken (friendship connections, relationships, etc).

**Person:** [            ] [ Search ]

3. **In the search results that appear, find the person you want to block and click the Block Person link next to his name.**

# Reporting Violations

Facebook takes violations of its privacy policy seriously. The site makes reporting potential violations easy by displaying a Report link on every Facebook application page and next to virtually every potentially offensive bit of info members add to the site, from discussion threads to wall posts.

> **Note** "Offensive" can mean anything from pornographic to threatening. To see a list of what Facebook considers offensive, check out the site's Code of Conduct: *www.facebook.com/codeofconduct.php*.

In addition to getting upset by things other members post on walls or upload to their profiles, people sometimes find third-party applications (page 206) offensive. Examples of potentially offensive applications include those that revolve around a tasteless pastime (seeing how many nude photos you can upload, for example), those that don't work or work differently than advertised, or those you suspect of misusing your profile information.

To report an application:

1. **In the Application Directory (click Applications, and then click the Browse More Applications button), find the application you want to report, and then click the application's name.**

2. **On the application page that appears, click the Report Application link.**

3. **In the pop-up window Facebook displays, use the drop-down list to tell Facebook why you're reporting the application.** Type your comments into the text field, and then click the Report button.

**Report the application "SuperPoke!"**

You are about to report a violation of our Terms of Use. **All reports are strictly confidential.** This report will be logged and the developers will be contacted to take action as necessary.

Reason: Choose one...

Choose one...
Privacy violation
Inappropriate or pornographic content
Advertisement/Spam
Application does not work
Attacks individual or group
Drug use
Violence

Additional Comments: (required)

To report other abuses like threatening wall or discussion posts, or links to pirated content, surf to the offending post or other item and click the Report link next to it.

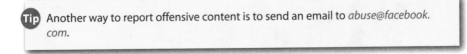

**Tip** Another way to report offensive content is to send an email to *abuse@facebook.com*.

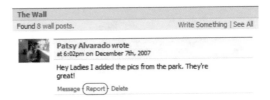

**Tip** For additional ideas to keep your info safe—including strategies for protecting your kids as they venture onto Facebook—scroll to the bottom of any Facebook screen and click the Help link. On the page that appears, click the Safety tab.

# 14

# Facebook Mobile

F acebook can be addictive. If you're away from a computer and feel
the need to check in on your Facebook friends or update your status, you can use *Facebook Mobile* on your cellphone to stay in the
loop. Whether you travel a lot or just like to stay connected when you're
between work and home, Facebook Mobile is a handy way to access Facebook without a computer.

# How Facebook Mobile Works

Facebook Mobile is an application (page 206) that lets you use your Internet-ready cellphone to:

- **Interact with Facebook on your phone's teensy-tiny screen.** Facebook's *Mobile Web* feature (page 247) lets you use the browser on your cellphone to see a scaled-down version of the Facebook Web site. Using your phone's keypad, you can do things like update your status, find out what your friends are doing, look up peoples' phone numbers, and keep tabs on the groups and events you've signed up for.

- **Interact with Facebook via text messages.** The *Mobile Texts* feature (page 248) lets you do things on Facebook from your phone *without* having to go through the mobile version of the Facebook Web site. (This option is usually faster than the Mobile Web feature, and is the way to go if your phone doesn't have a Web browser; you will, of course, need to be able to send text messages.) If you want to write a quickie message on a friend's wall, for example, you can text message a specific Facebook code (see page 248) along with your friend's name and your message.

- **Upload photos and video clips.** Perfect for posting impromptu additions to groups and events (as well as for tracking project updates), Facebook's *Mobile Uploads* feature (page 249) lets you sling the media clips you capture with your cameraphone or video phone directly to your Facebook account.

- **Subscribe to your friends' mobile uploads.** With the *Mobile Subscriptions* feature (page 250), you can sign up to have a notification sent to your cellphone when your friends upload new photos and video clips to their Facebook accounts.

> **Tip** If you own a Blackberry, check out the specially designed Facebook application "Facebook for Blackberry Smartphones". (See page 207 for help finding and installing this application.)

Like all Facebook applications, Facebook Mobile is free to use. But don't forget that every time you use Facebook Mobile, you're likely racking up charges on your cellphone bill. If your phone company charges you every time you use your phone to connect to the Web or send a text message, that means you pay every time you access the Facebook site or poke a Facebook friend via text message.

**Note** Facebook Mobile is great for quickie tasks like looking up profile info, checking event start times, and announcing your status. It's *not* so great for text-intensive tasks you occasionally do on Facebook, such as fleshing out your profile or writing a 12-page note.

# Setting up Facebook Mobile

Before you can use Facebook Mobile, you have to do a little bit of easy setup. You just need to activate your phone number, and then adjust your mobile settings; the following sections show you how.

**Note** Although Facebook Mobile is a Facebook application, you don't install it the way you do other Facebook applications (page 206). Instead, you have to follow the activation process explained in the next section. After that, Facebook lists Facebook Mobile in your Applications menu.

## Activating Your Phone

Activating your phone means associating a cellphone number with your Facebook account, and then testing the connection between your phone and Facebook. To activate your phone:

1. **At the top right of any Facebook screen, click the "account" link.** Then, on the page that appears, click the Mobile tab.

2. **On the Mobile tab, type your cellphone number into the Phone Number field.** Include your country and area code, but leave out the punctuation, like dashes and parentheses.

3. **From the Carrier drop-down list, choose your cellphone company, and then click the Activate button.** Facebook redisplays the Mobile tab, complete with a message letting you know you'll receive a confirmation code on your phone shortly.

4. **Check your cellphone.** It may take a few minutes for the text message with your confirmation code to arrive. If you don't get a text message from Facebook after 15 minutes or so, hit your browser's back button and make sure you typed in your cellphone number correctly.

| Settings | Networks | Notifications | Mobile |
|----------|----------|---------------|--------|

**Confirmation sent.**
A confirmation code has been sent to your phone.

**Activate a Phone**

Activating allows Facebook Mobile to send text messages to your phone. You can receive notifications for friend requests, messages, wall posts, and status updates from your friends.

You can also update your status, search for phone numbers, or upload photos and videos from your phone.

1.956.555.1212 on AT&T pending  resend code | remove

Confirmation code:

[                    ]  [ Confirm ]

**Mobile Web**

Browse Facebook from your phone, optimized for your mobile device.
Go to **m.facebook.com** on your phone's internet browser. Learn More.

Go to Facebook Mobile »

5. **Type your confirmation code into the "Confirmation code" field, and then click Confirm.** After you do, Facebook displays a successful activation message across the top of a page you can use to edit your mobile settings. The Mobile application appears in your Applications menu, and you can start interacting with Facebook using your cellphone. It's a good idea to edit your mobile settings before you get started, though; see the next section for details.

**Confirmed!**

Facebook Mobile is now activated. Text '@' followed by a message to FBOOK (32665) to update your status. You can also receive texts when people poke, message, wall post, or friend you. The Mobile application has also been added to your Facebook profile.

**Mobile Texts**

**Texts are:**

◉ On ○ Off

**Which texts should go to my phone?**

☑ Pokes — sent by Everyone ▾

☑ Messages — sent by Everyone ▾

☐ Comments — on — Mobile Uploads ▾

> **Note** If you don't see a congratulatory message after you type in your confirmation code, make sure you typed the code correctly (capitalization counts). If you still can't get it to work, zip to the top of the Mobile page and click the Help link. Then, on the Mobile help page, scroll down to the Troubleshooting portion of the Mobile Web section and click the "This isn't working on my phone" link. Doing so displays a message with a "here" link; click the link to pop up a message box you can use to contact Facebook for personalized help.

**Please tell us more...**

Your name and email address will be automatically submitted.

Subject: Mobile Web Not Working

Cell Phone Number: 19565551212

Mobile Service Provider: AT&T

Type of phone that you are using:

A detailed description of your problem:

Send   Cancel

# Adjusting Your Settings

You'll want to adjust your Facebook Mobile settings right after you activate your phone because these settings affect the type, number, and timing of text messages you receive from your Facebook friends. (You may not appreciate getting 50 pokes at 3 a.m. from your cut-up night-owl friend Bob, for example—especially if you have to pay for them.)

To customize your mobile settings:

1. **Head to the "edit mobile settings" page.** Facebook automatically displays the page after you finish activating your phone (see page 243). Or, if you surfed away from that page, in the Applications menu, click Mobile; on the Mobile page that appears, click the Edit Mobile Settings button.

> **Note** The "edit mobile settings" page doesn't actually say "edit mobile settings" across the top; instead, it just says "Mobile" (which is unfortunate, because all the other pages in the Mobile application say the same thing). You know when you're looking at the "edit mobile settings" page because you see a bunch of settings you can tweak.

2. **On the "edit mobile settings" page, use the checkboxes, radio buttons, and drop-down lists to tell Facebook what kinds of text messages you want to receive.** When you finish, click Save Preferences.

What times should texts be sent to my phone?

⦿ Anytime ⦾ Only from [10AM ▾] to [2AM ▾]

How many texts should be sent?

Limit my daily texts to [unlimited ▾]

☐ Do not text me while I am logged in

Should a confirmation text be sent when I poke, message, or wall post from my phone?

⦾ Yes ⦿ No

**My Phone**

Send texts to: [▓▓▓▓▓▓ ▾] manage phones

Facebook does not charge for this service. However, AT&T's normal text messaging rates still apply.

[ Save Preferences ] [ Cancel ]

# Using Facebook Mobile

After you've activated at least one cellphone *and* tweaked your mobile settings, you're ready to use Facebook Mobile. The following sections show you how.

## Surfing Facebook from Your Phone

To view and interact with a scaled-down version of Facebook specially designed for cellphones, point your cellphone to the Web site *http://m.facebook.com* and log in with your regular Facebook login and password. (Exactly how you get to the site depends on the cellphone you're using; check your phone's manual for instructions.)

**Note** If you own an iPhone, head to the iPhone-optimized version of Facebook at *http://iphone.facebook.com*.

You can do almost as much on the mobile version of Facebook as you can on the regular version. But the kinds of things you probably want to do (and the things that are easiest to do using the hunt-and-peck method most people employ when using phones as personal computers) include:

- Viewing and changing your status
- Checking the status of your friends
- Searching for people
- Tracking your upcoming events
- Viewing your news feed
- Seeing recent group activity

# Interacting with Facebook via Text Message

Many of the quick, basic things you do on Facebook—updating your status, for example, or sending someone a message—can be accomplished more easily by sending a short text message from you cellphone than by using your phone's screen to browse and interact with the Facebook Mobile Web site.

To text message Facebook, send a message to 32665 (that's FBOOK for folks who prefer looking at the letters on the keypad, rather than the numbers). Table 14-1 shows you the different things you do on Facebook by text messaging 32665. If what you want to text has something to do with another Facebook member, make sure you type in the person's full name. (And depending on how common that name is, you might have to jockey with your cellphone a bit to make sure you reach the right person; see page 249.)

**Note** Texting Facebook isn't instantaneous: It can take anywhere from a few minutes to a few hours for your actions to appear on Facebook. When they do, Facebook text messages you to let you know (if you've told it to; see page 246).

*Table 14-1. Actions You Can Take by Text Messaging 32665 (FBOOK)*

| Action | Code | Text Message Example |
|---|---|---|
| Update your status | @ | **@** at a Halloween party |
| Search for somebody's profile info | srch | **srch** john doe |
| Get somebody's cell number | cell | **cell** john doe |
| Send a message to somebody | msg | **msg** john doe how did the interview go? |
| Poke somebody | poke | **poke** john doe |
| Post an ultra-silly, cellphone-only "on fire" notification (which, similar to a poke, appears on somebody's profile), as in "John Doe is *on fire*!" | fire | **fire** john doe |
| Post on somebody's wall | wall | **wall** john doe congrats on the new gig |
| Send a friend request to somebody | add | **add** john doe |
| Write a note | note | **note** having a great time in vegas |
| Get help on how to text Facebook | help | **help** |

# Uploading a Picture or Video

If you've got a cellphone that snaps pictures or shoots video, you can up-load your pictures or video clips straight to Facebook—*after* you do a little setup work. To upload pictures:

1. **Send a sample picture to Facebook.** From your cameraphone, send a picture as a multimedia message to *mobile@facebook.com* (exactly how you do this depends on your cellphone). In the subject line of your message, type a caption for your photo.

2. **If this is the first time you've uploaded a picture or video clip, wait for your confirmation code, and then type it into Facebook Mobile.** After Facebook receives your photo, the site text messages you a code that you need to give to the Facebook Mobile application. To do so: From the Applications menu, choose Mobile. Then, on the Mobile page that appears, scroll down to the Mobile Uploads section and click the "Enter a confirmation code" link. In the "Confirmation code field" that appears, type your code, and then click the Confirm button.

3. **Send more pictures.** After you complete step 2 above, you're good to go: You can upload pictures willy-nilly. The pictures you upload appear in the Mobile Uploads box that Facebook displays on your profile.

To upload video clips:

1. **Find and install the Video application.** Flip to page 207 for instructions on finding and installing applications.

2. **Upload videos from your phone.** Send your video clips as multimedia messages to *mobile@facebook.com*. In the subject line of your message, type a caption for your video clip; in the body of your message, type in a description. The video clips you upload appear in the Mobile Uploads box on your profile.

> **Note** If this is your first time uploading a media clip, you need to retrieve your confirmation number and type it into Facebook Mobile before you can upload additional clips (see page 249).

## Subscribing to Friends' Mobile Uploads

If you've got a friend who uploads a lot of pictures or videos from her phone, you can get a quick heads-up on your phone when she does by subscribing to your friend's mobile updates, like so:

1. **From the Applications menu on the regular Facebook Web site, choose Mobile.** Facebook displays the Mobile page.

> **Note** You can subscribe to your friends' mobile uploads from the Facebook Mobile site, too.

▤ **Mobile**                                                                ( + **Edit Mobile Settings** )

Your friends have not recently uploaded mobile content.

When your friends upload mobile photos they will appear here.

**Mobile Subscriptions**

Facebook Mobile allows you to subscribe to your
friends' mobile uploads by sending them as SMS links to
your phone.

Whose mobile uploads should go to my phone?

Start typing a friend's name

**Edit your mobile settings**

Learn more about Mobile Texts

▤ **Mobile Uploads**

Upload photos and videos straight to Facebook
from your phone. Send an MMS to:

**mobile@facebook.com**

Enter a confirmation code

**Mobile Web**

Browse Facebook from your phone's internet
browser. Go to:

**m.facebook.com**

Learn more about Mobile Web

2. **Scroll to the Mobile Subscriptions section and, in the text field, type your friend's name.** To save you some time, as you type, Facebook pops up a helpful list of suggestions; click your friend's name to select it. After you choose a name, you're subscribed. Facebook displays the name below the text field so you can remove it later, if you like.

> **Note** If, when you subscribe to a friend's mobile uploads, you see a message saying you can't get your subscription because texts are turned off, here's what to do: From the Applications menu, choose Mobile, and then click the Edit Account Settings button. On the page that appears, turn on the "Texts are: On" radio button, and then scroll down to the bottom of the page and click Save Preferences.

# Deactivating Your Phone

If you change your cellphone number or just change your mind about using Facebook Mobile, you can deactivate the service quickly and easily:

**Note** You don't have to wait until you get back to your computer to deactivate your phone; you can do it right from your phone using the Facebook Mobile site. Either way, simply follow the steps below.

1. **From the Applications menu, choose Mobile.** Then, on the Mobile page that appears, choose Account.

**Note** Here's another way to get to the Mobile tab: Head to the top of any Facebook screen and click the "account" link; then, on the page that appears, click the Mobile tab.

Mobile Uploads | Phonebook | (Account)

📱 **Mobile**

2. **On the Mobile tab that appears, find the phone number you want to deactivate and click the "remove" link next to it.** In the confirmation box that appears, click the Remove Phone button.

**Note** Sometimes cellphone numbers get reassigned, and nothing's more aggravating than receiving text messages you don't want (but that you may end up paying for). To stop receiving messages from Facebook, send a text message to 32665 (that's FBOOK) that includes the word STOP or OFF.

# APPENDIX

# Getting Help

**F**acebook is pretty easy to use—especially if you keep this book handy. But Facebook's design team regularly adds new features and changes existing ones. So, someday soon you may log in to Facebook and find a new menu option or discover that your favorite application doesn't work the way it used to. When that day comes, you can get up to speed quickly by checking Facebook's Help section or getting info from other Web sites that cover Facebook. Read on to learn more.

# Facebook Help

Unlike some online help pages, Facebook Help is easy to find, well-written, succinct—and usually helpful (imagine that). To access Facebook Help:

1. **Scroll to the bottom right of any Facebook screen and click the Help link.**

> **Tip** You can also find Help links in other places around the site, including at the top of all built-in Facebook applications (such as Photos, Groups, and Events). If you click one of these links, you'll jump directly to the Help page for that application.

2. **On the Help tab that appears, click the topic you want to know more about.** You can also type a phrase into the Search Help Topics text box and hit Return.

3. **If the Help topic you picked doesn't answer your question, click a different one.** If you just can't find what you're looking for, you can contact Facebook and ask for help, as explained in the next section.

| Help | Suggestions | Safety |
| --- | --- | --- |

**Help Topics**

Search Help Topics

**Core Features**
- News Feed and Status
- Profile and Mini-Feed
- The Wall
- Search
- Friends
- Inviting Friends
- Pokes
- Networks
- Pages
- Inbox and Messages
- Requests and Notifications
- Subscriptions
- Add and Edit Applications

**Account**
- Sign Up and Login Problems
- Account Settings
- Privacy and Security
- Copyright Policy
- Actions from External Websites

**Business Solutions**
- Social Ads
- Facebook Pages
- Developer Platform
- Polls
- Advertising with Flyers

**Applications by Facebook**
- Photos
- Events
- Groups
- Notes
- Posted Items
- Marketplace
- Video
- US Politics
- Gifts
- Mobile

**Known Site Problem**

**Group/Event Messaging**

Some groups and events are unable to mass message their members. We hope to resolve this issue as soon as possible. We apologize for any inconvenience.

# Contacting Facebook

Facebook sprinkles "click here to contact us" links liberally throughout the site (they usually appear near the bottom of a page). The wording of the link depends on where you are on Facebook; for example, in the Advertisers section of the site (page 177), the link reads "Contact our sales team". The one place these "contact us" links *always* appear is at the bottom of every Help screen. To contact Facebook:

1. **Click any of the Help topics on the Help tab (page 256).** You've probably already done this *and* read all the topics, but you still have a question—which is why you want to contact Facebook.

2. **Scroll to the bottom of the Help topic page and click the "Write us a message" link.** Up pops a dialog box you can use to send Facebook's customer service team a note. Bear in mind that Facebook has over 50 million members, so you might not receive a quick, personalized response.

How do I reactivate my account?

Still didn't find what you were looking for? Write us a message

# Useful Facebook-related Web Sites

Facebook's Help feature is the last word on how the site works, and its About section is the official source of press releases and other goings-on (click the About link at the bottom of any Facebook screen to get to it).

But sometimes the most useful information is the stuff that's *not* officially sanctioned. Here are a few of the meatiest sites around:

- **The Facebook Blog** (*http://blog.facebook.com*). Actually, this site *is* officially sanctioned, so keep that in mind. It contains updates, tips, and explanations written by people who work for Facebook. This is the place to go when you notice a new feature on Facebook (or discover that an old one is gone or working differently) and want to know why the Facebook designers made the change—and what you can expect next.

> **Tip** Don't want to type the addresses of these Web sites by hand? No problem. Head to *missingmanuals.com* and click the "Missing CD-ROMs" link in the upper-left part of the page. On the Missing CD-ROMs page, click the "Missing CD-ROM" link next to this book's cover. Voilà—a clickable chapter-by-chapter list of all the Web sites mentioned in these pages.

- **Inside Facebook** (*www.insidefacebook.com*). This independent blog tracks Facebook's evolving business model with a clear, critical eye. It's a good site to check out if you're using Facebook to advertise yourself or your company.

- **The Unofficial Facebook Blog** (*www.allfacebook.com*). This blog is a good place to read up on controversial Facebook issues and draw your own conclusions. It's great if you want to be in the know about Facebook.

- **People-powered Customer Service for Facebook** (*http://getsatisfaction.com/facebook*). You can find questions (and answers) about unexpected Facebook behavior on this unofficial discussion board. It's a great resource if you've got an email in to Facebook's customer service department and just can't wait until they get back to you.

# Index